Workbook for

Motorcycles

Fundamentals, Service, and Repair

by

John Hurt
Technical Writer

Publisher
THE GOODHEART-WILLCOX COMPANY, INC.
Tinley Park, Illinois

MW00845417

Important Safety Notice

Proper service and repair is important to the safe, reliable operation of motorcycles, ATVs, and scooters. Procedures recommended and described in this textbook are effective methods of performing service operations. Some require the use of tools specially designed for this purpose and should be used as recommended. Note that this textbook also contains various safety procedures and cautions, which should be carefully followed to minimize the risk of personal injury or the possibility that improper service methods may damage the engine or render the vehicle unsafe. It is also impor tant to understand that these notices and cautions are not exhaustive. Those performing a given service procedure or using a particular tool must first satisfy themselves that neither their safety nor engine or vehicle safety will be jeopardized by the service method selected.

This textbook contains the most complete and accurate information that could be obtained from various authoritative sources at the time of publication. Goodheart-Willcox cannot assume any responsibility for any changes, errors, or omissions.

Contents

			Text	Workbook
Chapter	1	Introduction to Motorcycles, ATVs, and Scooters	11	7
Chapter	2	Shop Safety and Environmental Protection	41	19
Chapter	3	Tools, Measuring Instruments, and Shop Equipment	49	25
Chapter	4	Fasteners, Gaskets, and Diagnostic Procedures	77	35
Chapter	5	Basic Electrical and Electronic Theory	101	43
Chapter	6	Engines	121	53
Chapter	7	Fuel Systems	145	65
Chapter	8	Battery and Charging Systems	183	75
Chapter	9	Ignition Systems	207	83
Chapter	10	Lubrication Systems	227	91
Chapter	11	Cooling Systems	245	101
Chapter	12	Exhaust Systems and Emissions Control	257	109
Chapter	13	Power Transmission Systems	273	117
Chapter	14	Wheels and Tires	305	127
Chapter	15	Brakes	327	135
Chapter	16	Frame and Suspension Systems	353	145
Chapter	17	Accessory Systems	379	157
Chapter	18	Engine and Power Transmission Disassembly	395	165
Chapter	19	Two-Stroke Engine Overhaul	409	175
Chapter	20	Four-Stroke Engine Overhaul	431	185
Chapter	21	Power Transmission Overhaul	463	197
Chapter	22	Tune-Up and General Service	485	207
Chapter	23	The Business of Motorcycle, ATV, and Scooter Service	507	217

Introduction

The **Workbook for Motorcycles, Fundamentals, Service, and Repair** is a supplemental textbook designed to reinforce your understanding of the important information supplied in the textbook. To accomplish this task, the workbook utilizes several types of questions and illustration exercises to highlight key aspects relating to the operation, construction, design, maintenance, troubleshooting, and repair of motorcycles, ATVs, and scooters.

As with the textbook, an objective is provided at the beginning of each chapter of the workbook to summarize what should be learned. Each question in every workbook chapter is presented in a manner that measures your comprehension and knowledge of the important topics. The workbook's illustration exercises provide visual learning tools to help you understand actual construction, maintenance, troubleshooting, and repair conditions and procedures.

The workbook units correlate with those in the textbook. The order of the questions follows the sequence of the textbook material. This will make it easier for you to find information in the textbook and also to check your answers. It is recommended that before you attempt to answer questions in this workbook, you should study the **Motorcycles** textbook first. After studying the textbook, try to answer as many of the workbook questions as possible without referring to the textbook. Answer any remaining questions by referring to the appropriate areas in the textbook chapter.

The basic purpose of the **Motorcycles** textbook is to help you become a successful motorcycle technician. The basic function of the workbook is to provide a study guide that reinforces your knowledge and understanding of the important information contained in the textbook.

John Hurt

Instructions for Answering Workbook Questions

Each chapter in this workbook directly correlates to the same chapter in the textbook. Before answering the questions in the workbook, study the assigned chapter in the textbook and answer the end-of-chapter Review Questions. Then, review the objectives at the beginning of each workbook chapter. This will help you review the important concepts presented in the chapter. Try to complete as many workbook questions as possible without referring to the textbook. Then, use the textbook to complete the remaining questions.

A variety of questions are used in the workbook including multiple choice, identification, completion, and short answer. These questions should be answered in the following manner:

Multiple Choice

Select the best answer and write the correct answer in the blank.

1. In an opposed-twin cylinder engine, the cylinders lay _____ to the motorcycle frame.

   A. horizontally

   B. at right angles

   C. vertically

   D. Both A & B.

1. _A_

Completion

In the blank provided, write the word or words that best complete the statement.

2. A motorcycle's rear wheel _____ provides a mounting place for the brake drum or brake disc and sprocket.

2. _axle_

Identification

Identify the components indicated on the illustration or photograph accompanying the question.

3. Identify the parts of the engine measurement procedure illustrated below.

A. _Outer ring set screw_

B. _Dial indicator_

C. _Roller locknut_

D. _Adapter locknut_

E. _Adapter_

F. _Roller_

G. _Piston head_

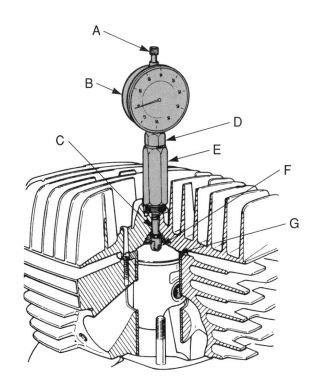

Short Answer

Provide complete responses to the statements.

4. Why is it important to keep hand tools free of oil and grease?

To prevent slippage that can cause injury; to have a professional appearance.

Other Types of Questions

When other types of workbook questions are presented, follow the specific instructions that accompany the problem.

Name _____

Date _____

Instructor _____

Period _____   Text pages 11-40

1

Introduction to Motorcycles, ATVs, and Scooters

Objective: After studying this chapter, you will be able to describe and explain the various types, designs, and operating systems of motorcycles, ATVs, and power scooters.

Instructions: After studying the textbook, answer the workbook questions.

The Role of Qualified Service Technicians

1. Why do modern motorcycles, ATVs, and scooters require well trained and qualified technicians to service them?

_____

_____

_____

_____

_____

2. _____ are fast becoming the workhorses for outdoor sports, agriculture, and home maintenance.

2. _____

3. _____ are the backbone of the quick delivery businesses in cities.

3. _____

4. What are the basic goals and qualifications of professional motorcycle service technicians?

_____

_____

_____

_____

_____

_____

_____

5. What are the professional duties of a motorcycle technician?

_____

_____

_____

_____

_____

_____

_____

_____

Styles and Designs of Motorcycles, ATVs, and Scooters

6. Name eight types of motorcycles.

_____

_____

_____

_____

7. *True or False?* Scooters can travel over 100 miles (160 km) on just   7. _____
   one gallon (3.8 L) of gasoline.

8. What type of motorcycle is shown in the photo below?

_____

Name _____

Engine

9. What is the function of a motorcycle's engine?

_____

_____

_____

10. Describe what an engine must do in order to operate.

_____

_____

_____

_____

_____

_____

_____

11. When an engine's piston moves down, a _____ is developed in
the cylinder.

11. _____

12. A four-stroke cycle engine requires four up and down piston
movements or strokes to complete _____.

12. _____

13. Describe the sequence of events in a four-stroke cycle engine.

_____

_____

_____

_____

_____

_____

_____

_____

14. During the _____, the piston slides down the cylinder while the
intake valve is open and the exhaust valve is closed.

14. _____

    A. intake stroke

    B. compression stroke

    C. power stroke

    D. exhaust stroke

15. What position are the engine valves at during the compression stroke?

_____

16. Where is the piston located during the power stroke?   16. _____

    A. Approaching BDC.

    B. At TDC.

    C. Approaching TDC.

    D. At BDC.

17. Identify the actions of the power stroke.

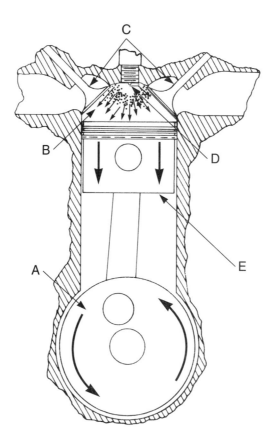

    A. _____

    B. _____

    C. _____

    D. _____

    E. _____

18. _____ helps to draw air and fuel into the cylinder, and aids in   18. _____
expelling the burned exhaust gases.

Name _____

19. Explain the function of an engine flywheel.

_____

_____

_____

_____

20. How many times does a two-stroke cycle engine produce power   20. _____
during each crankshaft revolution?

   A. 1.

   B. 2.

   C. 4.

   D. variable, depending on the speed of the engine.

21. All the following are characteristics of a two-stroke cycle engine,   21. _____
EXCEPT:

   A. two-stroke cycle engines have a power stroke every crankshaft
       revolution.

   B. two-stroke cycle engines pass their air-fuel mixture into the
       crankcase before reaching the combustion chamber.

   C. two-stroke intake and exhaust timing is controlled by the
       piston.

   D. two-stroke cycle engines use valves.

22. In a two-stroke cycle engine, air-fuel mixture enters the crankcase   22. _____
_____ the piston.

23. *True or False?* In a two-cycle engine, compression begins as soon   23. _____
as the exhaust port is blocked.

Engine Power Characteristics

24. Crankshaft rotation produces _____ and useful power.   24. _____

25. _____ is performed when an object is moved.   25. _____

26. _____ is the ability to perform work.   26. _____

27. Define the term *torque.*

_____

28. _____ is a measurement of the amount of work being completed.   28. _____

   A. Torque

   B. Power

   C. Energy

   D. Work

29. Explain the term *horsepower.*

_____

_____

Fuel System

30. Describe the function of an engine's fuel system.

_____

_____

31. All the following are parts of a motorcycle's fuel system, EXCEPT: 31. _____

   A. shutoff valve.

   B. combustion chamber.

   C. carburetor or injectors.

   D. air cleaner.

32. Explain the function of a carburetor.

_____

_____

33. A carburetor relies on _____ for operation.   33. _____

   A. pressure differences

   B. rider input

   C. venturi

   D. None of the above.

34. A _____ is a restriction formed in the carburetor throat.   34. _____

35. The _____ is connected to the carburetor butterfly or throttle slide.   35. _____

36. A(n) _____ is provided in the fuel system to keep airborne dirt from being carried into the carburetor and engine.   36. _____

37. How does electronic fuel injection eliminate the performance problems caused by lean carburetor settings?

_____

_____

38. What is the function of an electronic control module in an EFI system?

_____

_____

_____

Name _____

39. What is the air-fuel ratio in an EFI system?

    A. 15:1.

    B. 14.9:1.

    C. 3:1.

    D. 14.7:1.

39. _____

40. All the following are primary advantages an EFI system has over a carburetor fuel system, EXCEPT:

    A. provides a predetermined air-fuel mixture.

    B. it can compensate for worn parts.

    C. is able to make precise adjustments.

    D. provides fuel based on engine requirements.

40. _____

Electrical System

41. Many motorcycles use a _____ to store and supply electricity for initial starting, ignition, and lighting.

41. _____

42. All the following are typical components of a motorcycle's starting system, EXCEPT:

    A. battery.

    B. rectifier.

    C. starter motor.

    D. start switch.

42. _____

43. Explain the operation of a motorcycle's starting system.

_____

_____

_____

_____

44. A(n) _____ is used on most motorcycles to generate electrical current and voltage.

44. _____

45. What is the purpose of the charging system's rectifier?

_____

_____

46. A _____ is used to prevent battery overcharging.

46. _____

47. What normally powers the ignition system on most motorcycles?

_____

48. A(n) _____ is actually a step-up transformer that provides the high voltage for the ignition system.

_____

49. Explain the term *energy transfer ignition system.*

_____

_____

Cooling System

50. An air-cooled engine transfers heat directly into the air by means of _____.

50. _____

51. Which of the following is *not* a location for cooling fins on a two-stroke cycle engine?

    A. Cylinder.

    B. Cylinder heads.

    C. Exhaust pipes.

    D. Crankcases.

51. _____

52. The liquid-cooled engine transfers engine heat into _____.

52. _____

53. In a liquid cooling system, the _____ transfers heat into the outside air.

    A. cooling fins

    B. radiator

    C. thermostat

    D. fan

53. _____

54. What is the advantage of liquid cooling systems over air-cooled systems?

_____

_____

_____

_____

Lubrication Systems

55. What is the function of the engine lubrication system?

_____

_____

_____

Name _____

56. In a two-stroke cycle engine, lubricating oil passes through the engine with the _____.

   A. air-fuel mixture

   B. exhaust gas

   C. air

   D. fuel

56. _____

57. Which of the following is *not* a common four-stroke cycle lubrication system?

   A. Dry sump.

   B. Wet sump.

   C. Common sump.

   D. Splash sump.

57. _____

58. The _____ is the area where oil collects in the bottom of the engine.

58. _____

Exhaust System

59. Name the three functions of a motorcycle's exhaust system.

_____

_____

_____

60. What materials are used to make exhaust systems?

_____

_____

61. What is used to protect the rider from being burned on the hot exhaust pipe or muffler?

   A. Heat shield.

   B. Stainless steel.

   C. Chrome.

   D. Heat-resistant paint.

61. _____

Power Transmission

62. The power transmission in a motorcycle sends power from the engine crankshaft to the _____.

62. _____

63. What are the two main functions of a power transmission's primary drive?

_____

_____

64. A _____ is provided in the primary drive to engage and disengage   64. _____
power to and from the transmission.

    A. input shaft

    B. input gear

    C. clutch

    D. pushrod

65. Describe the function of a motorcycle's transmission.

_____

_____

66. Motorcycles and ATVs commonly have anywhere from _____ to   66. _____
_____ different speeds or ratios.

67. The _____ connects the transmission to the rear wheel(s).   67. _____

68. The final drive will generally have a reduction ratio of about: 68. _____

    A. 4.11:1.

    B. 3:1.

    C. 1:1.

    D. 8:1.

Chassis

69. The motorcycle frame provides a means of rigidly mounting the   69. _____
_____.

    A. engine

    B. suspension

    C. accessories

    D. All of the above.

70. The suspension system uses _____ and _____ to smooth the ride   70. _____
of a motorcycle.

71. The most common types of motorcycle suspension are composed   71. _____
of _____ on the front and a _____ with shock absorbers on the
rear.

Name _____

72. Identify the parts of the following motorcycle suspension system.

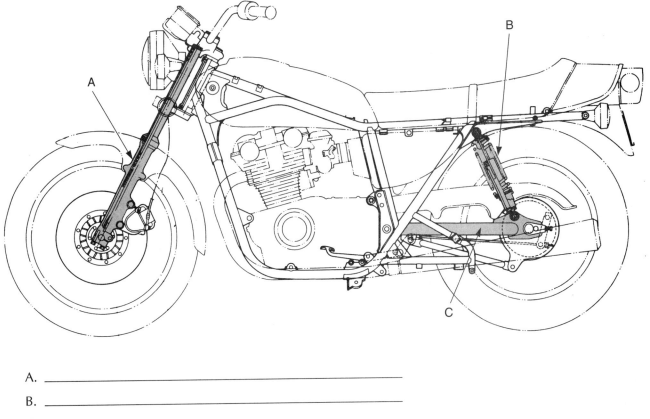

A. _____

B. _____

C. _____

Wheels and Tires

73. Describe the function of a motorcycle's wheel/tire assemblies.

_____

_____

_____

74. Why did manufacturers design a one-piece cast alloy wheel for modern motorcycles?

_____

_____

75. Explain the functions of motorcycle tires.

_____

_____

_____

Brakes

76. What is the purpose of motorcycle brakes?

_____

77. Name two common motorcycle brake designs.

_____

78. Name two newer brake systems.

_____

_____

Accessory System

79. Which of the following is *not* included in a motorcycle's accessory system?

    A. Starting system.

    B. Turn signals system.

    C. Warning lights system.

    D. Horn system.

80. Why are fuses utilized in an accessory system?

_____

_____

2

Shop Safety and Environmental Protection

Objective: After studying this chapter, you will be able to explain the importance of safety notices, shop safety, technician personal safety, and the use of fire extinguishers. Also, you will learn to detect possible hazardous waste in the shop area.

Instructions: After studying the textbook, answer the workbook questions.

Safety Notices

1. Explain the term *warning*.

   _____

   _____

   _____

   _____

2. What should be the technician's number one consideration when working with motorcycles, ATVs, and scooters?

   _____

   _____

Personal Safety

3. Why must you avoid working too fast when performing service procedures on a motorcycle?

   _____

   _____

   _____

4. Give an example of a possible hazard present in the repair shop.

_____

_____

_____

_____

5. All the following should *not* be worn in the shop, EXCEPT: 5. _____
   A. rings.
   B. goggles.
   C. ties.
   D. watches.

6. Explain the importance of wearing long pants in the shop repair area.

_____

_____

_____

_____

7. _____ is the most important part of the motorcycle technician's   7. _____
   uniform.

8. To prevent the absorption of solvent and other chemicals into your   8. _____
   skin while cleaning parts, wear a pair of _____.
   A. protective gloves
   B. bracelets
   C. open-toed shoes
   D. All of the above.

9. What protective equipment should be worn during operations involving drilling, grinding, or welding?

_____

_____

_____

_____

10. Why should you always keep the shop clean and organized?

_____

_____

_____

_____

Name _____

11. Never lay _____ on the floor as they can become lost or
damaged.

    A. tools

    B. parts

    C. engines

    D. Both A & B.

11. _____

12. What should you use to clean up oil on the shop floor?

    A. Water.

    B. Gasoline.

    C. Commercial oil absorbent

    D. Parts solvent.

12. _____

13. Where should you store oil and solvent soaked shop rags?

_____

_____

_____

_____

14. When should the shop ventilation fan be turned on?

_____

_____

_____

_____

15. Where should you store gasoline and other flammable materials?

_____

_____

_____

_____

16. Lift heavy parts using your _____.

    A. legs

    B. back

    C. arms

    D. None of the above.

16. _____

17. Never carry _____ or _____ in your pockets as they can easily
puncture your skin.

17. _____

18. Why is it important to wipe tools clean and dry after each use?

_____

_____

19. If welding or brazing on a motorcycle is required, remove the   19. _____
    _____ to a safe distance, at least 50 feet (15.24 m) away.

    A. fuel tank

    B. rear shocks

    C. fire extinguisher

    D. Both A & B.

20. During what service procedures should the motorcycle's battery be disconnected?

_____

_____

_____

21. Describe how to properly move a motorcycle around the shop area.

_____

_____

_____

Fire Prevention

22. Name the three conditions that must be present at the same place and time in order for combustion to occur.

_____

_____

_____

23. Most shops now have multipurpose _____ fire extinguishers that   23. _____
    are capable of fighting all three types of fires.

24. List the three basic types of fires. Also, explain how to extinguish each type.

_____

_____

_____

25. All the following are fire safety rules that should be followed in   25. _____
    any motorcycle shop, EXCEPT:

    A. never create flames or sparks near fuel.

    B. try to fight the fire until the fire department arrives.

    C. store volatile liquids in properly labeled containers.

    D. keep batteries away from sparks or flame.

Name _____

26. What procedures should be followed if a fire extinguisher cannot contain the fire after a short period of time, and the fire begins to spread?

_____

_____

_____

_____

Environmental Protection

27. Why is it important to handle and store oil, gasoline, solvents, and other chemicals properly?

_____

_____

_____

_____

28. A good policy to protect the environment is _____.

A. recover

B. repair

C. recycle

D. All of the above.

28. _____

29. A poor running motorcycle engine wastes fuel, increases wear, and increases _____.

29. _____

Exhaust Pollutants

30. What types of hazardous materials and waste are of most concern to the motorcycle technician?

_____

_____

_____

_____

31. Which of the following materials is considered hazardous waste?

A. Used engine oil.

B. Contaminated fuel.

C. Used gear oil.

D. All of the above.

31. _____

32. Testing for hazardous waste can be done by any qualified laboratory that performs tests on _____.

32. _____

33. The Occupational Safety and Health Administration (OSHA)
    Hazard Communication Standard publication was originally
    created for _____ who require their employees to handle
    potentially hazardous materials in the workplace.

    33. _____

34. What is the purpose of an MSDS?

    _____

    _____

    _____

    _____

35. It is important that any recycling equipment or recycling company
    is _____ approved.

    35. _____

3

Tools, Measuring Instruments, and Shop Equipment

Objective: After studying this chapter, you will be able to describe the types of tools, equipment, measuring devices, and part cleaning methods used in a motorcycle repair shop. You will also be able to explain the safety rules to follow when using these tools, devices, and cleaning methods.

Instructions: After studying the textbook, answer the workbook questions.

Tools and Equipment

1. Why should a motorcycle technician invest in good quality tools that are backed by a lifetime warranty?

_____

_____

2. List the categories of tools and equipment needed for the maintenance, service, and repair of motorcycles.

_____

_____

_____

_____

_____

Tool Boxes

3. In what part of a tool box are large power tools normally kept?   3. _____

    A. The roll-around cabinet.

    B. Upper tool box.

    C. Tote tray.

    D. None of the above.

4. Define the term *tool holders.*

_____

_____

_____

Hand Tools

5. Identify the following types of wrenches.

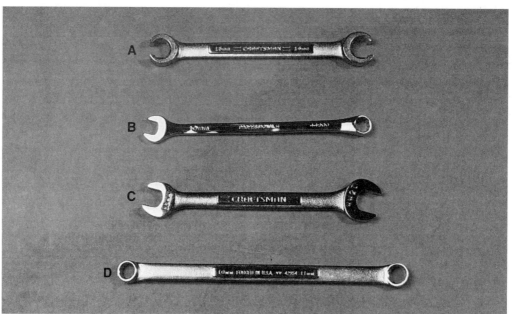

A. _____

B. _____

C. _____

D. _____

6. What type of wrench should be used on standard fasteners?   6. _____

7. A _____ is similar to a box-end wrench, but has a slot in the end.   7. _____

8. In motorcycle repair, a(n) _____ is a fill-in tool and is the least desirable of all wrenches.   8. _____

9. When loosening or tightening fasteners, always _____ rather than _____ the wrench.   9. _____

Name _____

10. Name two categories of screwdrivers commonly used for motorcycle repair.

_____

_____

_____

11. The most common _____ bit sizes used on motorcycles are   11. _____
    numbers 2 and 3.

12. What is the purpose of an impact driver?

_____

_____

_____

13. Why is it important to wear eye protection when using an impact driver?

_____

_____

_____

14. *True or False?* You should not hammer on screwdrivers.   14. _____

15. A _____ socket is short and is the most frequently used socket.   15. _____

16. A _____ socket is preferable to a 12-point socket since there is   16. _____
    less chance of rounding off the fastener head.

17. A(n) _____ is the most commonly used type of socket driver.   17. _____

18. What is the purpose of a breaker bar?

_____

_____

_____

19. What type of socket driver is depicted in the following illustration?

_____

_____

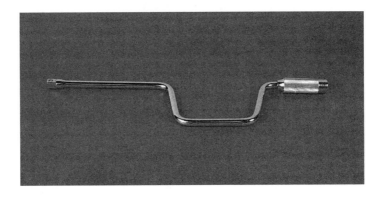

20. A(n) _____ allows the ratchet to drive the socket at an angle.   20. _____

    A. extension

    B. universal

    C. T-handle

    D. breaker bar

21. A(n)_____ increases the distance between the ratchet and the   21. _____
socket.

22. Which of the following best describes the function of pliers?   22. _____

    A. Pliers are used for hammering.

    B. Pliers are used for turning bolts.

    C. Pliers are used for pinching.

    D. Pliers are used for holding or gripping.

23. List the rules to follow when using Allen wrenches.

_____

_____

_____

24. The major difference in hammers is the _____ and the _____ of   24. _____
the head.

25. Identify this hammer.

_____

_____

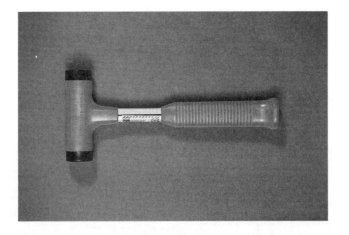

Name _____

26. Describe the purpose of files.

_____

_____

27. All the following are classifications for files, EXCEPT: 27. _____

   A. double cut.

   B. octarian cut.

   C. fine.

   D. coarse.

28. Large file teeth are for _____ materials.   28. _____

29. A _____ is used to clean a file.   29. _____

30. A(n) _____ punch is frequently used to mark parts for reassembly 30. _____
or for indenting parts before drilling.

31. A(n) _____ punch is used to drive shafts and bolts out of parts. 31. _____

32. _____ will exert high leverage for lifting or moving heavy or large 32. _____
parts.

33. _____ hacksaw blades are for cutting soft metals such as   33. _____
aluminum.

34. List six rules to follow to prolong hacksaw blade life and to avoid injury.

_____

_____

_____

_____

_____

_____

35. Explain the need for cleaning tools.

_____

_____

36. Power hand tools can be driven by either _____ or _____.   36. _____

37. Why should you use caution when using air tools?

_____

_____

38. Impact sockets are usually _____ in color.   38. _____

39. Why should a professional technician always use proper care and organization of his/her tools?

_____

_____

General Shop Equipment

40. *True or False?* General shop equipment is normally provided by the   40. _____
motorcycle repair facility.

41. _____ is used to diagnose and test the electrical systems of a   41. _____
motorcycle.

Measurement

42. The _____ measuring system uses random number indexes.   42. _____

43. The _____ system is a more consistent measuring system that uses   43. _____
scientific multiples of 10 to index all measurements.

44. _____ are only accurate to about 1/64 of an inch.   44. _____

       45. _____

45. A(n) _____ or _____ can be used as a straightedge to check part
alignment and for measurements not requiring extreme accuracy.   46. _____

46. A _____ is needed when the ruler must be held perfectly
square against the part being measured.   47. _____

47. Most outside micrometers are accurate to within _____.

48. Explain how to hold an outside micrometer during use.

_____

_____

_____

49. A(n) _____ micrometer will measure internal diameters and   49. _____
distances between surfaces.

50. A(n) _____ micrometer is used to measure the depth of a hole or   50. _____
recess in a part.

51. What is the purpose of a telescoping gauge?

_____

_____

Name _____

52. Name some common uses of a dial indicator.

_____

_____

_____

53. A(n) _____ feeler gauge will accurately measure flat, parallel surfaces.

53. _____

54. What type of gauge should be used to measure spark plug gap?

54. _____

55. _____ is a disposable measuring device made of thin strips of a clay-like substance.

55. _____

56. Describe the function of a compression gauge.

_____

_____

_____

57. What is normally indicated if a compression gauge reading is not within specifications?

_____

_____

_____

58. A _____ is used to determine exactly which parts inside a motorcycle engine might be causing low compression.

58. _____

59. Explain the function of a two-stroke cycle leak test.

_____

_____

_____

60. What are the most common uses for a vacuum gauge?

_____

_____

_____

61. A(n) _____ is used to measure valve spring and clutch spring tension.

61. _____

62. What should you do if a precision measuring tool is accidentally dropped or struck by some object?

_____

_____

Parts Cleaning

63. Identify the following piece of equipment.

_____

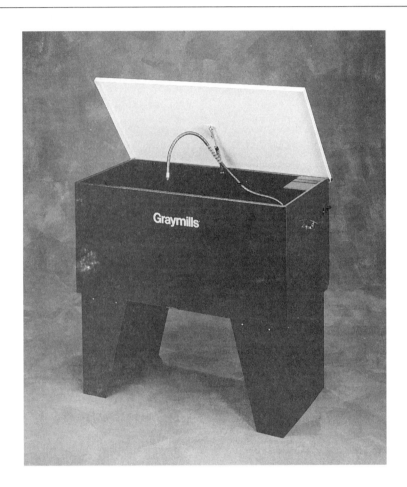

64. Describe the protective equipment that should be worn when using decarbonizing solvents.

_____

_____

_____

65. When using a wire wheel, always wear _____ and keep the _____ and shield in place.

65. _____

66. A _____ is used to remove gaskets, carbon, sludge, and sealing compounds from parts.

66. _____

Name _____

7. Define the term *dry-blast cleaning.*

_____

_____

_____

58. What are some of the applications of a dry-blast cleaner?

_____

_____

Special Operations

69. Explain the function of a boring bar.

_____

_____

70. List the important steps to remember when using a boring bar.

_____

_____

_____

_____

71. When would *resurfacing* be required on motorcycle parts?

_____

_____

72. What type of bench tool is depicted in the following illustration?

_____

73. Describe one of the applications of a hydraulic press during a motorcycle engine rebuild.

_____

_____

_____

74. A(n) _____ or _____ can be used to produce sufficient heat for   74. _____
    welding.

75. Name four types of welding used in motorcycle repair.

_____

_____

_____

_____

4

Fasteners, Gaskets, and Diagnostic Procedures

Objective: After studying this chapter, you will be able to identify and repair fasteners and threads. You will also learn how to properly use service manuals and perform diagnostic service procedures.

Instructions: After studying the textbook, answer the workbook questions.

Fasteners

1. Explain the term *fasteners.*

   _____

2. What determines the type of tool required to remove and install a   2. _____
   fastener?

   A. Fastener length.

   B. Fastener design.

   C. Fastener torque.

   D. All of the above.

3. Name the different classifications by which bolts and screws are identified.

   _____

   _____

4. The thread pitch of _____ bolts is determined by the number of   4. _____
   threads in one inch of threaded bolt length.

5. A bolt's _____ is the amount of stress or stretch it is able to   5. _____
   withstand.

6. With common _____ threads, the fastener must be turned   6. _____
   clockwise to tighten.

7. Nuts designed for motorcycle use are generally _____ in shape
   and are used on bolts and studs.

7. _____

8. What type of nut must be used with a grade 8 bolt?

   _____

9. Describe how studs are used to hold parts together.

   _____

   _____

10. Explain how to use a sheet metal screw.

    _____

    _____

    _____

11. All the following are rules to follow when replacing self-locking
    fasteners, EXCEPT:

11. _____

    A. use only new fasteners of the same type.

    B. install them to prevailing torque.

    C. reuse old fasteners.

    D. do not crossthread the fastener.

12. When using lock washers with die cast or aluminum parts, a(n)
    _____ is frequently installed under the lock washer to prevent part
    damage.

12. _____

13. Label the names and characteristics of the following lockwashers.

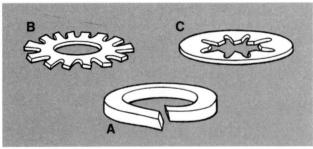

A. _____

B. _____

C. _____

Name _____

4. What problems can result if a motorcycle's fasteners are improperly torqued?

_____

_____

_____

5. When are thread repairs normally required?

_____

_____

_____

6. Name two useful tools for minor thread repairs.

_____

_____

7. A(n) _____ is used for external thread repairs.   17. _____

8. If a fastener is broken above the thread surface, _____ may be   18. _____
   used to unscrew the fastener.

   A. needle nose pliers

   B. flare-nut wrench

   C. channel locks

   D. locking pliers

19. What does installation of a thread repair insert involve?

_____

_____

_____

20. Dies are not frequently used in motorcycle repair since they cut   20. _____
    _____.

21. List in order the procedures that should be followed when tapping a new hole.

_____

_____

_____

22. Explain the rules to follow when using taps.

_____

_____

_____

23. All the following are methods of removing damaged nuts, EXCEPT: 23. _____

    A. applying cold.

    B. nut-splitter.

    C. chisel.

    D. hacksaw.

24. _____ are used both with slotted and castle nuts as well as on   24. _____
clevis pins and linkage ends.

25. Describe the purpose of snap rings.

_____

_____

26. Identify the following types of snap rings.

    A   **B**   **C**   **D**

    A. _____

    B. _____

    C. _____

    D. _____

27. _____ are used to both lock and position pulleys and other parts   27. _____
to shafts.

Gaskets and Seals

28. What type of materials are used to make gaskets?

_____

_____

_____

29. Explain the functions of a motorcycle's gaskets and seals.

_____

_____

_____

Name _____

30. Describe the purpose of a sealer.

_____

_____

31. _____ are used for semipermanent assemblies such as cover   31. _____
    plates, flanges, threads, hose connections, and other applications.

32. Define the term *form-in-place gasket.*

_____

_____

33. Name two common types of form-in-place gaskets.

_____

_____

34. Explain the function of seals.

_____

_____

35. How are seals constructed?

_____

_____

36. Which of the following is *not* a procedure for working with seals?   36. _____

    A. Use a seal driver to install the seal.

    B. Both the inside diameter (id) and outside diameter (od) must be
       the same.

    C. Compare the old seal to the new seal by holding them next to
       each other.

    D. Coat the inside of the seal with an approved sealer.

37. A(n) _____ is a stationary seal that fits into a groove between two   37. _____
    parts.

38. All the following are applications of adhesives on late-model   38. _____
    motorcycles, EXCEPT:

    A. hold body moldings.

    B. adhere engine covers.

    C. hold plastic and rubber parts.

    D. hold body emblems.

Using Service Manuals

39. What information is contained in a service manual?

_____

_____

_____

40. Name three types of service manuals.

_____

_____

_____

41. What type of information is normally contained in the repair sections of a motorcycle service manual?

_____

_____

_____

42. When should a service manual troubleshooting chart be used?

_____

_____

_____

43. Which of the following is *not* a step to follow when using a
    manufacturer's service manual or general repair manual.

    A. Locate any service manual.

    B. Turn to the table of contents or the index.

    C. Read the procedures carefully.

    D. Study the manual illustrations closely.

43. _____

44. _____ help the technician stay up-to-date with recent technical
    changes, repair problems, and other service related information.

44. _____

45. What is the purpose of an owner's manual?

_____

_____

_____

Name _____

Diagnostic Procedures

46. What is the first step in diagnosing a motorcycle problem?

    A. Fixing the problem.

    B. Verifying the problem exists.

    C. Documenting the repair.

    D. Verifying the problem is corrected.

46. _____

47. To ask the right questions, the service writer or technician should use a(n) _____.

47. _____

48. Why is it important for the technician or service writer to check a motorcycle carefully before performing a test ride?

    _____

    _____

    _____

49. When you know what the problem is, when it occurs, and what the operating conditions of the bike are, you are ready to narrow the possible causes down to a(n) _____.

49. _____

50. Define the term *symptom*.

    _____

    _____

    _____

51. List the three categories of troubleshooting problems.

    _____

    _____

    _____

52. Which of the following questions should be asked when troubleshooting a problem?

    A. What is the symptom?

    B. What system is involved?

    C. Where is the most logical place to begin diagnosis?

    D. All of the above.

52. _____

53. List in order the seven steps of troubleshooting.

_____

_____

_____

_____

_____

_____

_____

54. Which of the following would make troubleshooting easier?   54. _____

    A. Having all information possible about the bike's symptoms.

    B. Finding out when the problem first occurred.

    C. The service history of the bike.

    D. All of the above.

55. What four guidelines should a motorcycle technician follow when troubleshooting a problem?

_____

_____

_____

_____

5

Basic Electrical and Electronic Theory

Objective: After studying this chapter, you will be able to describe and explain the basic principles of electricity and electronics. Also, you will be able to identify basic electrical and electronic components and apply your knowledge of electricity and electronics to motorcycle repair.

Instructions: After studying the textbook, answer the workbook questions.

Electrical Theory

1. _____ are tiny particles of negatively charged matter that freely move about in an orbit around a nucleus.

    A. Electrons

    B. Protons

    C. Neutrons

    D. All of the above.

1. _____

2. Define the term *electricity.*

_____

_____

_____

3. Name several kinds of energy that are strong enough to force electrons out of their shells and cause electrical flow.

_____

_____

_____

_____

4. _____ and _____ are the two sources of energy that produce electricity in a motorcycle, ATV, and scooter.

4. _____

5. The _____ states that current flows from negative to positive.

5. _____

6. Name the two types of current used in motorcycle and similar vehicle electrical systems.

_____

_____

7. The majority of motorcycle, ATV, and scooter electrical systems use _____ current.

7. _____

8. _____ current is produced by the motorcycle's alternator.

8. _____

9. What does a simple circuit consist of?

_____

_____

_____

_____

10. The _____ feeds electricity to the conductors and load.

10. _____

11. _____ carry the electricity to the loads and back to the source.

11. _____

   A. Electrons

   B. Conductors

   C. Loads

   D. None of the above.

12. A(n) _____ circuit has all of the components connected one after the other with a single path for current flow.

12. _____

13. Why are all circuits on a motorcycle considered *one-wire circuits*?

_____

_____

_____

_____

Name _____

14. Identify the following types of electrical circuits.

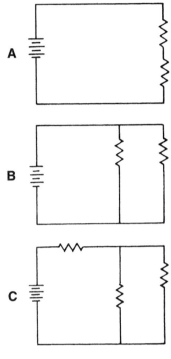

A. _____

B. _____

C. _____

15. Define the term *polarity*.

_____

_____

16. _____ is the pressure that forces free electrons to flow in a   16. _____
conductor.

17. _____ is measured with an ohmmeter in units called ohms.   17. _____

    A. Voltage

    B. Power

    C. Amperage

    D. Resistance

18. Explain the term *amperage.*

_____

_____

19. If a 12-volt circuit has a resistance of 3 ohms, what is the amount of current in this circuit?

_____

_____

_____

20. A circuit with 12 volts and 6 amps should have how much resistance?

20. _____

21. What is the formula for *voltage drop?*

21. _____

    A. $E = I \times R$

    B. $E = I \div R$

    C. $E = R \times I$

    D. $E = R \div I$

22. If you are installing a 30 watt taillight bulb on a motorcycle, and the maximum available voltage is 14 volts, what size fuse would be needed for this circuit?

_____

23. If a motorcycle is equipped with a 12-volt radio which draws 6 amps, how much wattage is used?

_____

24. A(n) _____ is caused when an exposed wire or connector touches ground, causing excess current flow.

24. _____

25. Explain the function of a fuse.

_____

_____

26. A(n) _____ is an electric switch that allows a small amount of current to control high current.

26. _____

    A. relay

    B. fuse

    C. circuit breaker

    D. solenoid

27. Explain how a solenoid operates.

_____

_____

_____

_____

Name _____

Motorcycle Electronics

28. Name three electronic operating systems used on a motorcycle.

_____

_____

_____

29. A(n) _____ is a special substance capable of acting as both a
conductor and an insulator.

    A. circuit breaker

    B. fuse

    C. semiconductor

    D. solenoid

29. _____

30. A(n) _____ is an electronic check valve that allows current to flow
in only one direction.

30. _____

31. Explain how a Zener diode operates.

_____

_____

_____

32. What is the function of a transistor?

_____

_____

33. What type of transistor is shown here?

_____

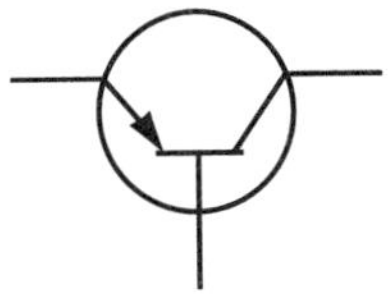

34. A(n) _____ contains almost microscopic diodes, transistors,
resistors, and capacitors in a wafer-like chip.

34. _____

Sources of Electricity

35. A battery stores electricity and provides a steady supply of _____ 35. _____
current for use in the motorcycle's electrical system.

36. A 12-volt motorcycle battery has _____ cells. 36. _____

    A. two

    B. six

    C. twelve

    D. three

37. _____ is the force that controls the operation of such components 37. _____
as the flywheel magneto, alternator or generator, ignition coils,
starter motor, and most mechanical relays.

38. If a wire cuts through a magnetic field, _____ will be induced in 38. _____
the wire.

Motorcycle Wiring

39. Define the term *primary wire.*

_____

_____

40. Why is primary wire insulation color coded?

_____

41. A(n) _____ is a plastic or tape covering that helps protect and 41. _____
organize the wiring on a motorcycle.

42. Wire size is determined by the diameter of the wire's _____. 42. _____

43. _____ has extra thick insulation for carrying high voltage from the 43. _____
ignition coil to the spark plugs.

44. _____ is extremely large gage wire capable of carrying high 44. _____
currents from the battery to the starting motor.

    A. Battery cable

    B. Solenoid wire

    C. Primary wire

    D. Secondary wire

45. Ground wires connect electrical components to the motorcycle 45. _____
_____.

Name _____

Electrical Schematics and Symbols

46. What is the function of a wiring schematic?

_____

_____

_____

47. *True or False?* All schematics are drawn the same.   47. _____

Electrical System Maintenance and Testing

48. Name some of the applications of a jumper wire.

_____

_____

49. What is the function of a test light?

_____

50. A voltmeter is normally connected to the circuit in _____.   50. _____

A. series

B. parallel

C. series-parallel

D. All of the above.

51. What is the purpose of an ammeter?

_____

52. Ammeters must be connected in _____ with the circuit being   52. _____
tested.

53. Describe the function of an ohmmeter.

_____

54. To prevent damage, an ohmmeter must *never* be connected to a   54. _____
source of _____.

55. Define the term *multimeter.*

_____

_____

Basic Electrical Diagnostic Methods

56. List four troubleshooting steps that apply to all electrical repair situations.

_____

_____

_____

_____

_____

_____

57. Explain how to use a voltmeter to measure circuit voltage.

_____

_____

_____

58. What is indicated if no voltage is present at a component when the measurements are taken directly from its input terminals?

_____

_____

59. The resistance value of an ignition coil indicates if it is _____ or   59. _____
    _____.

    A. normal

    B. malfunctioning

    C. firing

    D. Both A & B.

60. A continuity check indicates if a _____ is intact or broken.   60. _____

61. Describe how to calibrate an ohmmeter.

_____

62. What could be the possible problems if the resistance of an exciter coil are not within specifications?

_____

_____

63. When it is necessary to check current, remember that the ammeter   63. _____
    is always connected in _____ and it measures the current flowing
    through the circuit.

    A. series

    B. parallel

    C. series-parallel

    D. All of the above.

Name _____

64. Describe how a soldering gun is used to fasten wires.

_____

_____

_____

65. _____ solder should be used on all electrical repairs.   65. _____

66. _____ allow a wire to be connected to an electrical component.   66. _____

67. _____ allow a wire to be connected to another wire.   67. _____

68. _____ are used to deform the connector or terminal around the   68. _____
wire.

69. List the rules to follow when installing a crimp-on connector.

_____

_____

_____

70. In order for heat-shrink tubing to work correctly, it is important to   70. _____
select the correct _____ for the wire being repaired.

6
Engines

Objective: After studying this chapter, you will be able to describe the operating principles, major parts, designs, and different classifications of two- and four-stroke engines used on motorcycles.

Instructions: After studying the textbook, answer the workbook questions.

Four-Stroke Engines

1. Identify the fundamental parts of a four-stroke engine.

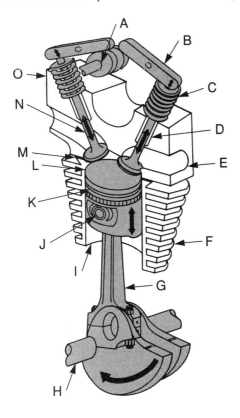

1. A. _____

B. _____

C. _____

D. _____

E. _____

F. _____

G. _____

H. _____

I. _____

J. _____

K. _____

L. _____

M. _____

N. _____

O. _____

2. A four-stroke engine requires _____ crankshaft revolutions for each power stroke.

2. _____

Valve Train

3. A(n) _____ is the most commonly used mechanism in current valve train design.

3. _____

4. What type of valve train design is normally used on touring bikes?

_____

Camshaft Arrangement

5. Explain how a motorcycle four-stroke engine's single overhead camshaft drive operates.

_____

_____

_____

_____

_____

6. With a four-valve engine, the _____ can be placed at the center of the combustion chamber, allowing good flame balance during combustion.

6. _____

7. Compared to the DOHC, the _____ engine is less expensive to manufacture and is easier to maintain due to a reduced number of parts.

7. _____

8. Define the term *valve float.*

_____

_____

9. Describe the purpose of valve springs.

_____

_____

10. What engine problems can result from *valve float?*

_____

_____

11. Camshaft _____ design determines when, how quickly, how long, and how far a valve opens.

11. _____

Name _____

12. Explain the term *camshaft lift*.

_____

_____

13. What is meant by the term *valve duration?*

_____

_____

Pistons, Crankshafts, and Cylinders

14. The piston and crankshaft assemblies are often termed the engine's   14. _____
_____.

15. Name some factors that determine the amount of horsepower and torque a four-stroke engine can produce.

_____

_____

16. What does a single cylinder motorcycle engine normally consist of?

_____

_____

_____

17. Explain the term *360° crankshaft*.

_____

_____

_____

18. In an opposed-twin cylinder engine, the cylinders lay _____ to the   18. _____
motorcycle frame.

   A. horizontally

   B. at right angles

   C. vertically

   D. Both A & B.

19. Why does a motorcycle equipped with opposed-twin cylinders have good handling characteristics?

_____

_____

20. Crankshafts for most V-twin engines have a common journal for   20. _____
both _____.

21. Multi-cylinder engines consist of _____ cylinders.

    A. three

    B. four

    C. six

    D. All of the above.

21. _____

22. Describe the construction of a modern motorcycle cylinder.

    _____

    _____

    _____

23. Explain the engine problems caused by a worn cylinder.

    _____

    _____

24. A motorcycle cylinder is normally designed so that it can be bored out to accept a(n) _____ piston.

24. _____

25. What is the most common piston construction method used on modern motorcycles?

    _____

26. _____ are best suited to high performance applications.

26. _____

27. Identify the parts of the following four-stroke cycle motorcycle piston.

A. _____

B. _____

C. _____

D. _____

E. _____

F. _____

G. _____

Name _____

28. A piston's _____ is directly exposed to the extreme heat and pressure caused by combustion.

28. _____

29. Why is a piston normally tapered?

_____

_____

_____

30. _____ pistons are machined out-of-round to provide dependable, quiet operation when the piston is both cold and hot.

30. _____

31. Define the term *piston slap.*

_____

_____

32. What is a combustion chamber?

_____

_____

33. A(n) _____ combustion chamber provides a very smooth dome-shaped chamber wall with very little surface area.

33. _____

34. Explain the term *side squish combustion chamber.*

_____

_____

_____

35. What type of combustion chamber is depicted in this illustration?

_____

_____

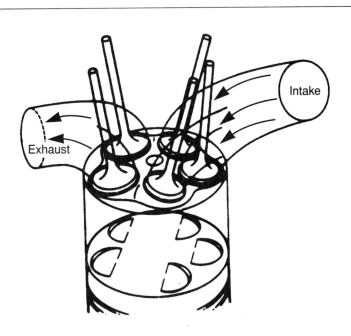

36. _____ are machined below the piston crown to hold the piston rings.

36. _____

37. Four-stroke pistons usually have _____ ring grooves.

37. _____

    A. three

    B. four

    C. six

    D. two

38. Name the two types of rings used on a four-stroke motorcycle piston.

_____

39. Describe the functions of piston rings.

_____

_____

_____

40. What are piston rings normally made of?

_____

41. Describe the purpose of a four-stroke piston's bottom ring.

_____

_____

_____

_____

42. The _____ ring is normally rectangular with the inside top edge chamfered.

42. _____

43. What is the function of a bearing?

_____

_____

44. Name the three types of bearings commonly used in a four-stroke engine.

_____

_____

45. _____ bearings provide the greatest reduction of friction.

45. _____

Name _____

Engine Case

46. What does a motorcycle engine case normally include?

_____

_____

_____

47. _____ consists of a separate engine and gearbox assembly.

47. _____

48. _____ utilizes a single case or crankcase casting that contains the engine, primary drive, and transmission.

48. _____

49. Most single cylinder four-stroke motorcycle engine crankcases are _____ split.

49. _____

50. What are the advantages of horizontal split cases?

_____

_____

_____

Two-Stroke Engine

51. Define the term *intake timing.*

_____

_____

_____

52. A(n) _____ engine uses piston skirt length and intake port location to control intake timing.

52. _____

53. Define the term *mild timing.*

_____

_____

_____

54. _____ timing will give more top end power but will sacrifice some midrange and low end power.

54. _____

55. Reed valve operation is dependent on crankcase _____ and _____.

55. _____

56. Explain the term *rotary valve*.

_____

_____

57. How does a rotary valve operate?

_____

_____

_____

58. A rotary valve is positioned between the _____ and the _____   58. _____
    and is keyed or splined to the engine crankshaft.

59. The _____ controls transfer and exhaust timing in two-stroke   59. _____
    engines.

Transfer and Exhaust Timing

60. Transfer and exhaust timing are usually determined by _____.   60. _____

61. Recent engine design allows for adjustable exhaust timing through   61. _____
    the use of _____.

Crankcase Sealing

62. What is used to draw the air-fuel mixture from the carburetor to the crankcase in a two-stroke engine?

_____

63. In a two-stroke engine, _____ is used to transfer air-fuel mixture   63. _____
    from the crankcase to the upper cylinder.

64. Name some of the locations a two-stroke engine is sealed.

_____

_____

_____

_____

_____

Name _____

Crankshaft Configurations

5. Label the names of the parts of the following single cylinder
crankshaft.

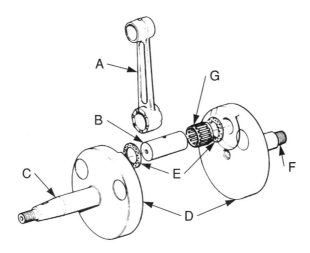

A. _____

B. _____

C. _____

D. _____

E. _____

F. _____

G. _____

66. A(n) _____, two-stroke crankshaft is simply two single cylinder   66. _____
crankshafts constructed side-by-side.

67. Identify the following type of motorcycle crankshaft.

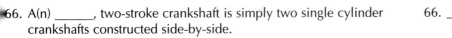

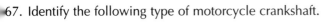

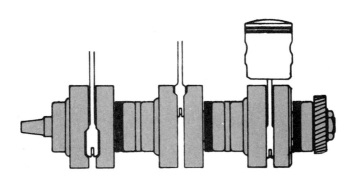

Piston and Ring Design

68. Which of the following is *not* a characteristic of a two-stroke piston?

    A. Transfer cutouts below the piston pin boss.

    B. Locating pins in the ring grooves.

    C. Oil control ring.

    D. Needle bearings between the piston pin and rod small end.

68. _____

69. Define the term *transfer cutouts.*

_____

_____

_____

70. Why are two-stroke engine pistons equipped with ring locating pins?

_____

_____

_____

_____

71. Why can piston expansion be a problem in a two-stroke engine?

_____

_____

_____

72. Two-stroke engines are designed to use either _____ piston rings.

    A. one

    B. two

    C. three

    D. Both A & B.

72. _____

73. Name the three ring designs used in two-stroke engines.

_____

_____

_____

Name _____

Cylinder Construction

74. The _____ for a two-cycle engine is normally a cast iron liner machined to fit tightly into an aluminum cylinder block.

74. _____

75. What is a disadvantage of a cast-in-sleeve two-stroke cylinder construction?

_____

_____

_____

76. Explain some of the advantages of the coated bore cylinder.

_____

_____

77. Piston rings pass a two-stroke engine's exhaust and transfer port windows twice during each _____.

77. _____

78. Why is it necessary for a two-stroke engine's port windows to be shaped properly?

_____

_____

_____

Vertical and Horizontal Split Crankcases

79. Most single cylinder two-stroke engines have _____ split crankcases.

79. _____

80. Twin and multiple cylinder two-stroke engines are normally split _____.

80. _____

7

Fuel Systems

Objective: After studying this chapter, you will be able to understand the basic operating principles and construction of both carburetors and electronic fuel injection systems.

Instructions: After studying the textbook, answer the workbook questions.

Fuel System Parts

1. What materials are used to manufacture motorcycle fuel tanks?

_____

_____

2. List three methods in which motorcycle fuel tank petcocks can be operated.

_____

_____

3. What is normally used to hold the fuel line on its fittings?

_____

4. A(n) _____ is required on motorcycles having the fuel tank located too low for gravity flow to feed fuel to the carburetor.

4. _____

5. Name three classifications of motorcycle fuel filters.

_____

_____

6. In most cases, a motorcycle air filter is enclosed in a(n) _____ connected to the engine by a rubber boot.

6. _____

7. Explain how a motorcycle's throttle twist grip increases and decreases engine speed.

_____

_____

_____

_____

8. Identify the components of this throttle cable assembly and related parts.

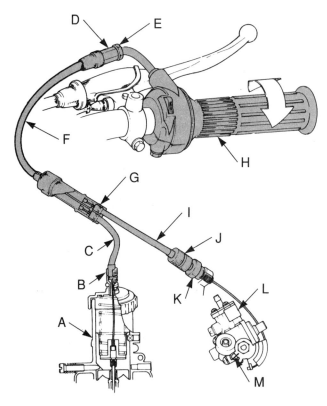

A. _____   H. _____

B. _____   I. _____

C. _____   J. _____

D. _____   K. _____

E. _____   L. _____

F. _____   M. _____

G. _____

Name _____

Gasoline

9. Gasoline is a compound of the elements _____ and _____ and is   9. _____
distilled from crude oil.

10. Define the term *octane rating.*

_____

_____

11. Name three additives that are blended into distilled gasoline at the refinery.

_____

_____

_____

12. What is the purpose of *oxygenated gasoline?*

_____

_____

13. What is the usual cause(s) of most motorcycle gasoline-related fuel system problems?

_____

14. _____ on acceleration is an indication that the fuel is either low   14. _____
quality or does not have the proper octane rating for the application.

Carburetors

15. What is the function of a motorcycle carburetor?

_____

_____

16. Engine _____ is closely related to proper fuel metering and   16. _____
atomization.

17. Define the term *air-fuel ratio.*

_____

_____

18. When is an air-fuel ratio considered rich?

_____

19. Define the term *variable venturi carburetor.*

_____

_____

_____

20. What is the function of positive carburetor linkages?

_____

_____

21. Most two-stroke engines use _____ carburetors.   21. _____

22. A carburetor's _____ meters air and fuel at and slightly above idle.   22. _____

23. What is the function of a carburetor's off-idle circuit?

_____

_____

_____

24. Explain the purpose of the needle circuit.

_____

_____

25. Name the two types of needle circuits.

_____

_____

26. What does a carburetor's main fuel circuit use to meter fuel flow?

_____

_____

_____

27. Describe the purpose of the accelerator pump circuit.

_____

_____

_____

28. The function of the _____ is to prevent any hesitation by   28. _____
    providing extra fuel during sudden throttle openings.

29. A carburetor's _____ is used to prevent afterburn.   29. _____

30. Which of the following is *not* a type of carburetor starter circuit?   30. _____

    A. Choke system.

    B. Cold start injection system.

    C. Tickler (primer) system.

    D. Enrichment system.

31. Describe how a vacuum carburetor operates.

_____

_____

_____

Name _____

2. In a vacuum carburetor, the _____ is the primary means of controlling air flow through the carburetor.

32. _____

3. What controls venturi restriction in a vacuum carburetor?

_____

4. A vacuum carburetor's _____ controls the off-idle air-fuel mixture.

34. _____

5. The butterfly controlled carburetor uses a butterfly valve to control _____ through the venturi.

35. _____

6. Name the three circuits used in a butterfly carburetor to meter fuel.

_____

_____

_____

37. List some of the common carburetor adjustments required to maintain the proper air-fuel mixture during the service life of a motorcycle.

_____

_____

_____

_____

38. Engine _____ is adjusted by means of a throttle stop screw.

38. _____

39. Identify the adjustment mechanism.

39. A. _____

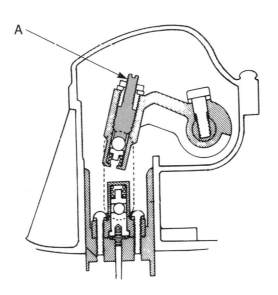

40. _____ refers to the level of fuel maintained in the float bowl.

40. _____

41. Why is throttle cable free play important?

_____

_____

_____

_____

42. Why are carburetor jet changes usually performed?

_____

_____

_____

_____

Carburetor Rebuilding

43. When is it necessary to rebuild a motorcycle carburetor?

_____

_____

_____

_____

44. What is normally used to attach the carburetor or carburetors to the motorcycle engine?

44. _____

   A. Sleeve.

   B. Spigot.

   C. Flange.

   D. All of the above.

45. Carburetor parts should always be placed in a _____ or _____ to prevent loss.

45. _____

46. How can you minimize the possibility of mixing parts when rebuilding multiple carburetors?

_____

_____

_____

47. What type of carburetor cleaning solvent should be used during a carburetor rebuild?

47. _____

Name _____

48. With the engine running, what final carburetor adjustments should be made after a rebuild?

_____

_____

_____

49. _____ should be reset after carburetor synchronization.   49. _____

Electronic Fuel Injection

50. What is the main advantage an EFI system has over a carburetor fuel system?

_____

_____

51. Name three functions of an EFI control module.

_____

_____

_____

52. What is the function of a CPU?

_____

_____

53. Explain the term *fall detection switch.*

_____

_____

54. Describe the function of an airflow meter.

_____

_____

_____

55. The function of the fuel injector is to spray the proper amount of   55. _____
fuel into the _____.

56. One injector is usually installed in the _____ of each of the   56. _____
motorcycle's cylinders.

57. What is normally used to regulate pressure in a motorcycle's EFI system?

_____

_____

58. Explain what a motorcycle's EFI system usually consists of?

_____

_____

_____

_____

59. The length of time the EFI injectors are open is determined by _____ from all the sensors.

59. _____

60. The intake pressure sensor converts the _____ to electrical signals.

60. _____

61. The _____ is used to compensate for air density changes in a motorcycle EFI system.

61. _____

62. The coolant temperature sensor signal is used by the _____ to set fuel injection pulse width based on engine temperature.

62. _____

63. _____ convert the temperature of the air entering the engine to electrical resistance.

63. _____

64. The throttle position sensor converts the physical angles of the _____ to electrical signals.

64. _____

65. Explain how a motorcycle's oxygen sensor operates.

_____

_____

_____

_____

_____

_____

Engine Control System Operation

66. The fuel injection period, injection timing, and ignition timing are controlled by the _____.

66. _____

67. How does an engine integrated control system decrease exhaust emissions?

_____

_____

_____

_____

Name _____

68. What is the theoretically correct air-fuel ratio?   68. _____

    A. 14.7:1.

    B. 13:1.

    C. 15:1.

    D. 3:1.

ECM Self-Diagnostics

69. What is indicated if an EFI warning light system blinks every .5-1 second?

_____

_____

_____

70. Explain the procedure to follow if a motorcycle's ECM is found to be defective.

_____

_____

Name _____

Date _____

Instructor _____

Period _____ Text pages 183-206

8

Battery and Charging Systems

Objective: After studying this chapter, you will be able to understand how to properly maintain the two types of batteries used in motorcycles. Also, you will be able to perform service tests on ac and dc charging systems.

Instructions: After studying the textbook, answer the workbook questionss.

Batteries

1. Define the term *electrolyte*.

_____

_____

2. The principle hazards in servicing batteries occur under _____ or when handling _____.

2. _____

3. Identify the parts of this motorcycle battery.

3. A. _____

B. _____

C. _____

D. _____

E. _____

F. _____

G. _____

H. _____

I. _____

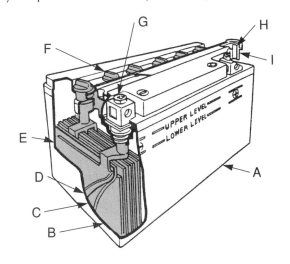

4. Explain the term *specific gravity* as it relates to electrolyte.

_____

_____

_____

5. A battery's electrolyte level goes down when water in the battery cells _____.

5. _____

6. What should you do if electrolyte gets in your eyes?

_____

_____

7. What is the function of battery *built-in sensors?*

_____

_____

8. How does a maintenance-free battery produce water for its cells?

_____

_____

_____

_____

_____

9. Maintenance-free batteries have _____ designed to open when excessive gas is produced.

9. _____

10. Which of the following is *not* part of normal motorcycle battery service?

10. _____

   A. Topping off battery cells with electrolyte.

   B. Cleaning the battery.

   C. Checking electrolyte specific gravity (when possible).

   D. Visual inspection.

11. When removing a conventional motorcycle battery, the _____ tube should be removed.

11. _____

12. Why is it important to always keep the top of a battery clean?

_____

_____

_____

13. _____ are the whitish-gray material that clings to the plates and battery case.

13. _____

14. _____ is contaminant or actual plate material that has settled to the bottom of the battery case.

14. _____

Name _____

15. What type of solution should be used to clean a battery case and terminals?

_____

_____

16. At what level should the electrolyte level be at on batteries with transparent cases?

_____

_____

17. Why should you *not* use tap water to refill the cells of a battery?

_____

_____

18. What are the common causes of battery mossing?

_____

_____

19. An unloaded battery test is made on a battery without _____
current.

19. _____

20. What is the primary function of a battery load and unloaded test?

_____

_____

21. The specific gravity readings from each of a battery's cells are 1.260 or higher and are within .050 of each other for all cells. What is indicated?

_____

_____

22. Name the conversion factors that should be used when checking a battery's specific gravity when the weather is extremely hot or cold.

_____

_____

_____

_____

_____

23. A maintenance-free battery's stabilized open circuit voltage is below 12.4 volts. What does this indicate?

_____

24. Describe how to perform a *load test* on a motorcycle battery.

_____

_____

25. The battery in a 12-volt system with a light load should have at least _____ volts.

25. _____

26. A motorcycle battery in a 6-volt electrical system with a light load should have at least _____ volts.

26. _____

27. A motorcycle battery's _____ rating measures the battery's ability to discharge current for an extended period of time.

27. _____

28. A battery's _____ rating indicates how well the battery can be expected to perform in low temperatures.

28. _____

29. To prevent damage to maintenance-free batteries, never remove the _____.

29. _____

30. A battery is said to be overcharged when excess _____ is supplied to the battery.

30. _____

31. What should the specific gravity of electrolyte be when it is poured into a new conventional battery?

31. _____

   A. 1.000.

   B. 1.150.

   C. 1.225.

   D. 1.265.

32. Describe the rules to follow when routing a battery vent tube during battery installation.

   _____

   _____

   _____

33. Explain the procedures to follow when installing a motorcycle battery.

   _____

   _____

   _____

   _____

   _____

34. Name five reasons why batteries fail.

   _____

   _____

   _____

   _____

   _____

Name _____

Alternators

35. What is used to control voltage flow in a motorcycle electrical system which uses an alternator that produces electricity mechanically?

_____

_____

36. Why are rectifiers used in a motorcycle charging system?

_____

_____

37. A motorcycle alternator is usually mounted on and driven by the _____.

37. _____

38. An alternator's _____ consists of a crankshaft driven flywheel with a series of magnets attached.

38. _____

39. The alternator's _____ consists of wire coils wound around a series of soft iron poles.

39. _____

40. Define the term *electromagnetic induction.*

_____

_____

_____

41. The _____ alternator is the most common type of alternator with the stator placed inside the rotor.

41. _____

42. The _____ alternator has low output and is best suited for small displacement engines and small electrical loads.

42. _____

43. What type of motorcycle would use an electromagnet alternator?

43. _____

_____

_____

44. What type of motorcycle normally uses a flywheel magneto?

_____

_____

_____

45. A true magneto is a self-contained _____.

45. _____

46. Identify the parts of the following flywheel magneto.

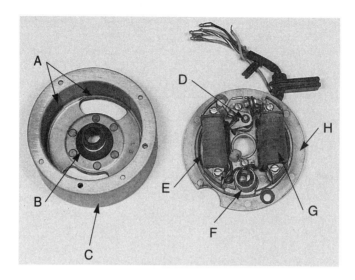

A. _____   E. _____

B. _____   F. _____

C. _____   G. _____

D. _____   H. _____

Dc Generators

47. Dc generators are rarely used on _____ motorcycles.   47. _____

Charging System Rectification and Regulation

48. Define the term *rectifier.*

_____

_____

_____

49. A(n) _____ is an electronic component that only allows current   49. _____
    flow in one direction.

50. A(n) _____ will allow current to flow in one direction, but will not   50. _____
    permit flow in the opposite direction if the voltage is below a
    certain point.

Name _____

51. A _____ only allows half of the alternator output to reach the battery.

51. _____

52. _____ are used to provide full alternator output conversion to dc for battery charging.

52. _____

53. What is the purpose of using a voltage regulator?

_____

_____

_____

54. Electronic regulators are used in both _____ and _____ charging systems.

54. _____

55. Explain the term *electronic regulator.*

_____

_____

_____

56. When an electronic regulator is used in an electromagnetic charging system, it matches _____ to the battery's needs by controlling alternator field voltage.

56. _____

Charging System Service

57. What is the first step that should be taken when a charging system defect is suspected?

_____

_____

58. What is the purpose of a parasitic draw test?

_____

_____

_____

59. List the procedure to follow when performing a parasitic draw test.

_____

_____

_____

_____

_____

_____

60. During a charging system _____ test, a high capacity ammeter is used to measure charging system amperage.

    60. _____

61. What is the function of a stator continuity test?

    _____

    _____

    _____

62. Explain what is indicated if the resistance values are found to be much higher than the specified values during a charging coil test.

    _____

Electric Starting Motor

63. Motorcycle electric starting motors use _____ current from the _____ for starting.

    63. _____

64. Explain how a motorcycle's electric starting motor circuit operates.

    _____

    _____

    _____

65. What is normally used to engage and disengage a motorcycle's starting motor?

    _____

    _____

    _____

9

Ignition Systems

Objective: After studying this chapter, you will be able to explain the basic operating principles, parts and construction of contact point, magneto, and electronic motorcycle ignition systems.

Instructions: After studying the textbook, answer the workbook questions.

Ignition Systems

1. Describe the function of a motorcycle's ignition system.

   _____

   _____

2. Most motorcycle ignition systems are powered by the _____.   2. _____

3. What component in a motorcycle's ignition system is used to step-up battery voltage?

   _____

   _____

4. A motorcycle's ignition system switching device is driven by the   4. _____
   _____ or _____.

5. Name three causes of resistance to spark plug operation.

   _____

   _____

   _____

   _____

6. _____ refers to the amount of voltage and duration of the spark at   6. _____
   the spark plug.

7. What components are part of a battery-powered ignition system primary circuit?

_____

_____

_____

_____

8. All of the components using battery voltage are included in an   8. _____
   ignition system's _____ circuit.

9. Identify this motorcycle ignition system trigger device.

_____

10. Name the three possible locations of a motorcycle's ignition system switching device.

_____

_____

11. A motorcycle ignition system's ignition coil is a simple _____   11. _____
    transformer.

12. An ignition system secondary circuit includes all the components   12. _____
    that operate on _____.

13. Ignition combustion must begin near the end of the _____ stroke,   13. _____
    before _____.

Name _____

14. Name three methods used to advance the ignition spark in a motorcycle engine.

_____

_____

_____

15. Under heavy engine load, vacuum _____ and timing _____. 15. _____

16. _____ advance systems require no mechanical advance and have 16. _____
no mechanical parts to wear.

17. Define the term *frequency of spark.*

_____

_____

_____

18. A four-stroke cycle engine requires an ignition spark in each 18. _____
cylinder for every 720° of _____ rotation.

19. Why do all two-stroke cycle engines require a separate ignition system for each cylinder?

_____

_____

20. Define the term *spark plug heat range.*

_____

_____

21. A spark plug is removed from a motorcycle's engine. The plug's ceramic insulator is clean and a light brown
color. What does this indicate about this particular plug's heat range?

_____

_____

22. What are some of the problems caused by carbon build-up on a spark plug?

_____

_____

23. What problems can result if a plug with an improper heat range is installed in a motorcycle's engine?

_____

_____

24. If plug reach is too _____, carbon will build up on the plug hole 24. _____
threads in the cylinder head, causing overheating and making it
very difficult to insert the correct spark plug later.

25. The spark plug _____ is an important factor in conducting the 25. _____
heat from the plug to the cylinder head.

26. Label the parts of the following spark plug.

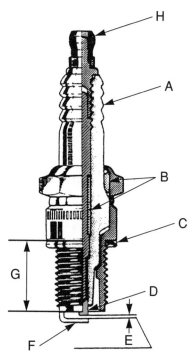

A. _____

B. _____

C. _____

D. _____

E. _____

F. _____

G. _____

H. _____

Types of Ignition Systems

27. What is the function of a condenser in a contact point ignition system?

_____

_____

_____

28. Define the term *electronic ignition*.

_____

_____

_____

Name _____

29. List the parts of a typical transistorized ignition system.

_____

_____

_____

30. Identify the ignition system shown below.

_____

31. Describe how a transistorized ignition system operates.

_____

_____

_____

_____

_____

32. Name two types of magnetic triggering devices used in electronic ignition systems.

_____

_____

33. Name the basic parts of a flywheel magneto ignition system.

_____

_____

_____

34. What produces the current in a flywheel magneto ignition system?

_____

_____

_____

35. Name two types of flywheel magneto ignition systems used on motorcycles.

_____

_____

_____

36. The digitally controlled transistorized ignition system controls   36. _____
    ignition timing using an _____ inside the spark unit which
    calculates the ideal timing at all engine speeds.

37. List the parts of a digitally controlled transistorized ignition system.

_____

_____

_____

38. Describe how a capacitor discharge ignition controls coil operation.

_____

_____

_____

39. A _____ is similar in appearance to a conventional flywheel   39. _____
    magneto.

40. Define the term *thyristor.*

_____

_____

_____

41. _____ in a _____ ignition system is caused by the change in   41. _____
    trigger coil voltage rise time as engine speed increases.

Name _____

Ignition Problems

2. A faulty ignition system is often related to _____.   42. _____

3. Name six ignition system problems that would cause a no-start or hard-start problem.

_____

_____

_____

_____

_____

_____

44. List five ignition system problems that would cause a motorcycle engine to run poorly at low speeds.

_____

_____

_____

_____

_____

45. A motorcycle engine knocks or produces abnormal engine noise. What possible ignition system problems can cause these engine conditions?

_____

_____

_____

_____

Name _____

Date _____

Instructor _____

Period _____ Text pages 227-244

10 Lubrication Systems

Objective: After studying this chapter, you will be able to describe and explain the different types and characteristics of motor oil. Also, you will be able to compare and service both two-stroke and four-stroke motorcycle engine lubrication systems.

Instructions: After studying the textbook, answer the workbook questions.

Oil

1. _____ is the resistance to movement between two touching parts.

1. _____

2. Which of the following is *not* a function of lubricating oil?

   A. Lubricates moving parts.

   B. Filters dirt and metal particles.

   C. Dissipates heat.

   D. Seals.

2. _____

3. Oil between a motorcycle's _____ and _____ aids in preventing combustion pressure leakage.

3. _____

4. Describe four types of lubricating oils suitable for use in motorcycle engines.

_____

_____

_____

_____

5. _____ is the ability of an oil to remain between two lubricated parts, preventing metal-to-metal contact.

5. _____

6. _____ refers to the thickness of an oil and is determined by the rate of oil flow under controlled conditions.

   A. Viscosity

   B. Film strength

   C. Detergent

   D. Foaming

6. _____

7. As oil heats up in an engine, it gets _____.

7. _____

8. How does *foaming* affect engine oil performance?

_____

_____

9. _____ keep unwanted products such as metal particles suspended in the oil so they may be drained during an oil change.

9. _____

10. Name the two organizations responsible for the testing and classification of oils.

_____

_____

11. All motor oils for use in _____ have a code beginning with the letter *S.*

11. _____

12. What is the rating of the current highest quality motor oil?

   A. SG.

   B. SH.

   C. SI.

   D. SJ.

12. _____

13. What does it mean if an oil is labeled *EC-II?*

_____

_____

14. Define the term *viscosity rating system.*

_____

_____

15. A 40 weight oil is _____ and will pour _____ than a 30 weight oil.

15. _____

16. _____ has the advantages of both high and low viscosity oils.

16. _____

Name _____

Two-Stroke Engine Lubrication

7. In a two-stroke engine, lubricating oil passes through the engine with the _____.

17. _____

8. How does a two-stroke premix lubrication system operate?

_____

_____

_____

9. Oil fed directly to a motorcycle's intake port is referred to as _____.

19. _____

0. Identify the parts of this motorcycle oil injection lubrication system.

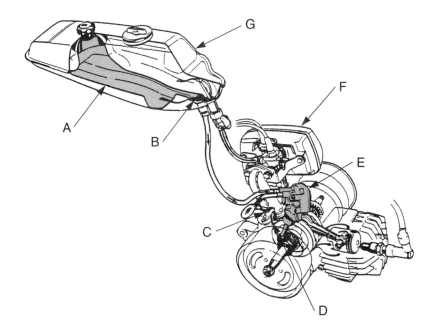

A. _____

B. _____

C. _____

D. _____

E. _____

F. _____

G. _____

21. _____ provides undiluted oil directly to the motorcycle engine's   21. _____
    main and connecting rod bearings.

22. What controls pump operation in a motorcycle's oil injection system?

    _____

    _____

    _____

23. Describe how to adjust a throttle cable on a motorcycle's oil injection pump.

    _____

    _____

    _____

    _____

24. Oil injection pump cable adjustment is accomplished by turning   24. _____
    a(n) _____ which varies the length of the outer oil pump cable
    housing.

25. _____ is required whenever air enters the feed line or oil injection   25. _____
    pump.

    A. Rebuilding

    B. Replacement

    C. Bleeding

    D. Both A & B.

26. Name five ways air can enter an injection system's oil supply line.

    _____

    _____

    _____

    _____

    _____

27. How is a motorcycle oil tank vented?   27. _____

    A. A small vent hole in the tank cap.

    B. A vent line attached to the top of the oil tank.

    C. A valve in the tank itself.

    D. Both A & B.

Name _____

8. _____ are sometimes used in a motorcycle engine's oil feed lines to allow flow in only one direction.

28. _____

29. Motorcycle oil injection systems are provided with either a(n)._____ or a(n) _____ oil filter.

29. _____

30. A(n) _____ is commonly used for primary drive and gearbox lubrication in two-stroke engines.

30. _____

Four-Stroke Engine Lubrication

31. A(n) _____ constantly circulates the same oil throughout the parts of a four-stroke engine.

31. _____

32. A typical dry sump lubrication system consists of all the following parts, EXCEPT:

32. _____

   A. a large sump.

   B. oil tank.

   C. oil pump.

   D. oil return line.

33. How does wet sump lubrication differ from dry sump lubrication?

_____

_____

_____

34. Define the term *spray system.*

_____

_____

_____

_____

35. Define the term *common sump lubrication.*

_____

_____

_____

36. Motorcycles that do not have a common sump design use sealed _____ that have their own oil supply.

36. _____

37. Identify the parts of the following gear type oil pump.

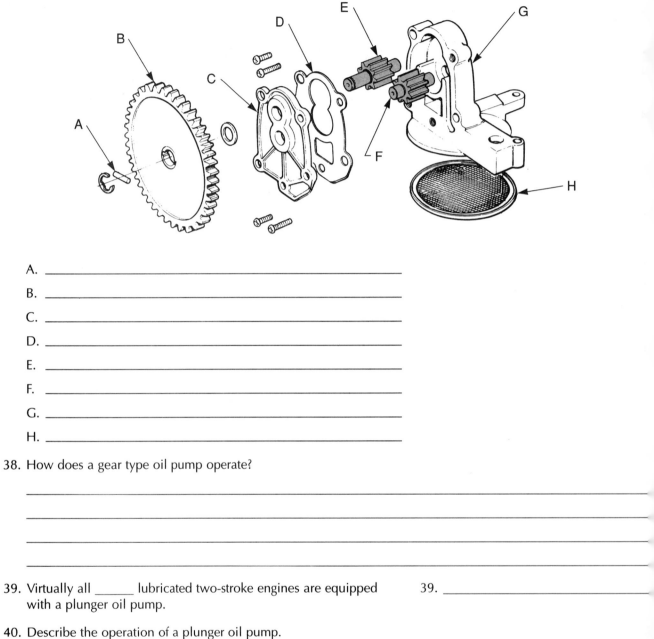

A. _____

B. _____

C. _____

D. _____

E. _____

F. _____

G. _____

H. _____

38. How does a gear type oil pump operate?

_____

_____

_____

_____

39. Virtually all _____ lubricated two-stroke engines are equipped with a plunger oil pump.

39. _____

40. Describe the operation of a plunger oil pump.

_____

_____

_____

_____

_____

_____

Name _____

41. Name the parts of a rotor oil pump.

_____

_____

_____

42. A rotor oil pump is the most common oil pump design used on _____ motorcycle engines.

42. _____

43. Explain how a rotor oil pump operates.

_____

_____

_____

_____

_____

44. A _____ is a device used to control maximum oil pressure in a motorcycle engine lubrication system.

44. _____

45. Describe the function of an oil filter in a motorcycle engine lubrication system.

_____

_____

_____

46. List two types of oil filters commonly used in motorcycle engines.

_____

_____

47. What type of engine oil filters are depicted in the illustration below?

_____

_____

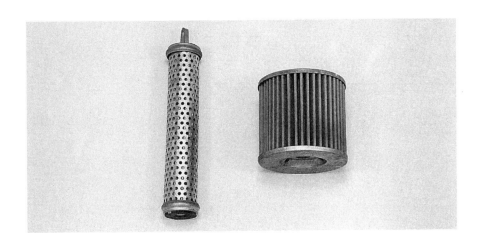

48. Name some of the inspection and service procedures that should be performed on an engine oil cooler.

_____

_____

_____

_____

49. Label the names of the parts of the following oil filter and
    bypass valve.

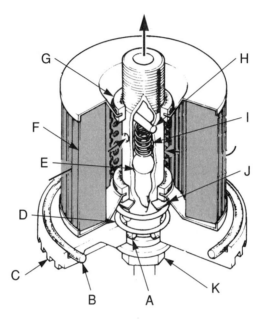

A. _____

B. _____

C. _____

D. _____

E. _____

F. _____

G. _____

H. _____

I. _____

J. _____

K. _____

Name _____

Lubrication System Maintenance

50. Explain the procedures to follow when checking the oil level in a typical four-stroke engine equipped with either a wet or dry sump.

_____

_____

_____

_____

_____

51. Some motorcycle engine models contain an oil level inspection window that allows the technician to visually check the oil level without using a _____.

51. _____

52. Describe one of the easiest and most accurate ways to locate the source of a motorcycle engine oil leak.

_____

_____

_____

53. How long after a motorcycle is purchased should the owner wait to change the engine oil?

53. _____

    A. 100 miles (160 km).

    B. 200 miles (320 km).

    C. 3000 miles (4800 km).

    D. 600 miles (960 km).

54. When changing a motorcycle's engine's oil and filter, the engine should be at _____ temperature.

54. _____

55. How does contaminated oil affect motorcycle engine parts?

_____

_____

56. List the procedures to follow when checking the oil pressure in a typical motorcycle.

_____

_____

_____

_____

_____

Troubleshooting Lubrication Systems

57. What are the possible problems if a two-stroke engine with oil injection produces excessive smoke and has excessive carbon on the spark plugs?

_____

_____

58. Which of the following would cause excessive exhaust smoke and a heavy carbon buildup on the plug(s) on a two-stroke engine using premixed oil?

    A. Improper jetting for altitude, air temperature, and external conditions.

    B. Oil pump worn or damaged.

    C. Improperly mixed fuel.

    D. Both A & C.

58. _____

59. A two-stroke engine using premixed oil overheats. All the following could be the cause, EXCEPT:

    A. fuel-oil mixture too old.

    B. too much oil in fuel.

    C. poor quality premix oil.

    D. improper jetting for altitude.

59. _____

60. A four-stroke motorcycle engine has no oil pressure. What are some of the possible causes?

_____

_____

_____

11

Cooling Systems

Objective: After studying this chapter, you will be able to explain the differences between motorcycle air-cooled and liquid-cooled engines. Also, you will be able to identify the parts and troubleshoot and service these two types of engine cooling systems.

Instructions: After studying the textbook, answer the workbook questions.

Air-Cooled Engines

1. Explain the advantages and disadvantages of an air-cooled motorcycle engine.

_____

_____

_____

2. What is the purpose of finned cylinder head(s) on air-cooled   2. _____
   engines?

   A. To increase the outside surface area.

   B. To transfer enough heat away from the engine and into the air.

   C. To fill in space between the upper and lower halves of the frame.

   D. Both A & B.

3. Why are cooling demands for a two-stroke engine generally more critical than for a four-stroke engine?

_____

_____

_____

4. _____ fins dissipate heat more efficiently than cast iron fins and   4. _____
   are used more frequently.

Liquid-Cooled Engines

5. A liquid-cooled engine can maintain optimal engine operating   5. _____
   temperature while preventing _____.

6. What is the major advantage of a liquid-cooled engine over an air-cooled engine?

   _____

   _____

7. Why is liquid cooling ideal for small and medium displacement two-stroke motorcycle racing engines?

   _____

   _____

8. What advantages does antifreeze have over water?

   _____

   _____

Liquid-Cooled System Components

9. Engine coolant is normally a 50-50 mixture of _____   9. _____
   (or equivalent) and _____.

10. The effectiveness of _____ decreases with the accumulation of   10. _____
    rust or if there is a change in the mixing proportion during usage.

11. A radiator is basically a _____, transferring heat from the engine   11. _____
    to the air passing through it.

    A. heat exchanger

    B. tube

    C. series of fins

    D. tank

12. The radiator itself is a series of _____ and _____ that expose heat   12. _____
    from the coolant to as much surface area as possible.

13. All the following are factors that influence the efficiency of a   13. _____
    radiator, EXCEPT:

    A. the area and thickness of the radiator core.

    B. ambient air temperature.

    C. the percentage of coolant to water.

    D. the amount of coolant going through the radiator.

14. Most motorcycle radiator cores are made of _____.   14. _____

Name _____

15. How does crushed or twisted fins affect a radiator's efficiency?

_____

_____

16. If one-third or more of a radiator's fins are crushed or twisted, the   16. _____
fins should be _____.

17. Most radiators feature _____ or drain bolts that allow a technician   17. _____
to drain coolant from the system.

18. Describe the function of a motorcycle cooling system's reserve tank.

_____

_____

19. What is indicated if a reserve tank's coolant level is low after   19. _____
repeated filling?

A. There is excess water evaporation.

B. There is probably a leak in the cooling system.

C. The engine is overheating.

D. The wrong type of coolant is being used.

20. Why are motorcycle liquid cooling systems pressurized?

_____

_____

21. Describe the function of a motorcycle cooling system radiator cap.

_____

_____

22. Explain the function of a radiator cap's pressure and vent valves.

_____

_____

23. Why should you wait until the engine is cool before removing the   23. _____
motorcycle's radiator cap?

A. It may cause pressurized coolant to escape.

B. It can cause serious scalding.

C. It can cause major engine damage.

D. Both A & B.

24. Describe the operation of a motorcycle cooling system thermostat.

_____

_____

_____

25. List the function of a cooling system water pump.

_____

_____

_____

_____

26. Most motorcycle water pumps are of the _____ design, with a rotating paddle wheel impeller to move the coolant.

26. _____

27. Identify the operations and components of the following motorcycle cooling system thermostat. Also, use arrows to show coolant flow.

A. _____

B. _____

28. All the following are functions of a motorcycle cooling system fan, EXCEPT:

28. _____

   A. it forces air to flow through the radiator and around the engine.

   B. dissipates heat.

   C. raises engine temperature.

   D. maintains system performance under severe conditions.

29. The _____ on typical bikes will automatically start or shut down the cooling fan depending on the temperature of the coolant.

29. _____

30. Explain the primary function of a cooling system hose.

_____

_____

_____

_____

Name _____

Servicing and Troubleshooting Air-Cooled Systems

31. List the rules to remember to properly maintain a motorcycle engine's air cooling system.

_____

_____

_____

_____

Servicing Liquid-Cooling Systems

32. What does servicing motorcycle liquid cooling systems normally involve?

_____

_____

_____

33. List the procedures to follow when using a hydrometer to determine a cooling system coolant's freezing point.

_____

_____

_____

_____

_____

_____

_____

_____

34. Always check the coolant level with the motorcycle in a _____ on   34. _____
a flat, level surface.

35. Describe how to drain and replace a motorcycle's cooling system coolant.

_____

_____

_____

_____

_____

36. Explain how to remove all air from a motorcycle's cooling system.

_____

_____

_____

_____

37. What should be done if a motorcycle's cooling system shows evidence of rust, scale, or lime in the coolant?

_____

_____

_____

38. The majority of water pump failures are attributed to _____.   38. _____

39. Identify the parts encountered during motorcycle water pump removal.

A. _____

B. _____

C. _____

D. _____

E. _____

40. Describe the procedures used to remove and replace a motorcycle water pump.

_____

_____

_____

_____

_____

_____

_____

_____

Name _____

41. What should you look for when inspecting the condition of a motorcycle's cooling system hoses?

_____

_____

42. Explain what is indicated if there are rust stains around a cooling system's hose clamp.

_____

_____

Troubleshooting Liquid-Cooling Systems

43. What should you look for when inspecting a motorcycle cooling system for problems?

_____

_____

_____

_____

44. All the following are possible causes of high engine temperature, EXCEPT:

    A. faulty radiator cap.

    B. insufficient coolant.

    C. faulty temperature gauge or gauge sensor.

    D. air in system.

44. _____

45. Which of the following would cause a motorcycle's engine temperature to be too low?

    A. Faulty temperature gauge or gauge sensor.

    B. Thermostat stuck open.

    C. Faulty cooling fan motor switch.

    D. All of the above.

45. _____

Name _____

Date _____

Instructor _____

Period _____ Text pages 257-272

12

Exhaust Systems and Emissions Control

Objective: After studying this chapter, you will be able to describe the operations and construction of a modern motorcycle exhaust and emission control system. You will also be able to explain the troubleshooting and service procedures for these systems.

Instructions: After studying the textbook, answer the workbook questions.

Exhaust Systems

1. All the following are functions of a motorcycle exhaust system, EXCEPT:

   A. reduce engine exhaust noise.

   B. aid in engine emission control.

   C. decrease engine horsepower.

   D. route burned exhaust gases to the rear of the motorcycle.

1. _____

2. What are motorcycle exhaust systems normally made of?

   _____

   _____

   _____

3. Why is a heat shield sometimes used over the outer side of a motorcycle exhaust system?

   _____

   _____

   _____

4. A street bike normally has the exhaust system located close to the _____.

4. _____

System Descriptions

5. Name the parts of a typical four-stroke exhaust system depicted in the illustration below.

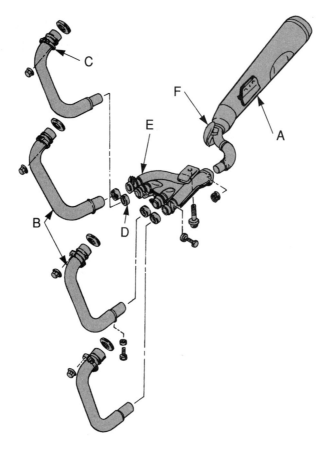

A. _____

B. _____

C. _____

D. _____

E. _____

F. _____

6. Define the term *exhaust pulse scavenge effect.*

_____

_____

_____

Name _____

7. Identify the parts of the following motorcycle muffler.

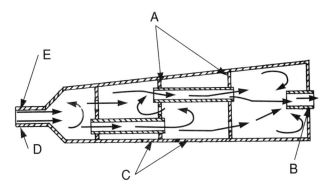

A. _____

B. _____

C. _____

D. _____

E. _____

8. When the exhaust valve opens, the exhaust gas flows rapidly from the port into the _____.

8. _____

9. What is the function of a two-stroke exhaust system's expansion chamber?

_____

_____

10. In two-stroke engine exhaust systems, a scavenging effect is used to help pull burned gases out of the _____.

10. _____

11. For best two-stroke engine performance, the expansion chamber must be compatible with the _____ of the engine.

11. _____

12. Which of the following is *not* a tool that can be used to pull small to medium size dents out of a motorcycle's exhaust system?

12. _____

   A. Prybar.

   B. Suction cups.

   C. Sheet screw and vise grips.

   D. Slide hammer.

13. What should a motorcycle exhaust system inspection consist of?

_____

_____

_____

_____

_____

14. Explain how a four-stroke motorcycle engine's exhaust ultimate power valve system operates.

_____

_____

_____

_____

_____

15. The muffler used on conventional four-stroke multicylinder motorcycle engines use a(n) _____ for each cylinder.

15. _____

16. Name two types of modern motorcycle exhaust pipe configurations.

_____

_____

17. Identify the following exhaust system arrangements.

_____

18. Explain the term *spark arrester.*

_____

_____

19. Describe how to clean most motorcycle exhaust pipes/mufflers.

_____

_____

_____

Inspecting and Servicing Exhaust Systems

20. List the rules to follow when installing a motorcycle exhaust system.

_____

_____

_____

_____

_____

Name _____

21. Name the two common problems with a typical motorcycle exhaust system and their causes.

_____

_____

_____

Turbochargers

22. What is another name for a turbocharger?

_____

_____

23. A turbocharger is a(n) _____ compressor.   23. _____

24. How does turbocharging affect a motorcycle's performance?

_____

_____

25. *True or False?* Turbochargers are available as a bolt-on kit.   25. _____

26. Why are motorcycle manufacturers not currently producing a model equipped with a turbocharger?

_____

_____

Emission Control Systems

27. All the following are products of the engine's combustion cycle,   27. _____
    EXCEPT:

    A. oxygen.

    B. hydrocarbons.

    C. carbon monoxide.

    D. oxides of nitrogen.

28. Why is it necessary to control a motorcycle engine's production of hydrocarbons?

_____

_____

29. What is indicated if a motorcycle engine produces higher-than-normal HC readings?

_____

_____

30. Name the possible causes of a high CO reading?

_____

_____

31. A high _____ reading indicates there is too much air in the
    mixture, not enough fuel, or the engine is running too hot.

31. _____

32. Name and explain the two emission control systems used in many recently produced motorcycles.

_____

_____

_____

_____

_____

_____

33. Identify the parts of the roll-over valve.

A. _____

B. _____

C. _____

D. _____

E. _____

34. An evaporative emission control system's roll-over valve must be
    located in a _____ position.

34. _____

35. A motorcycle engine's catalytic converter is located ahead of the
    _____ in the exhaust system.

35. _____

Name _____

36. What is the function of a motorcycle's catalytic converter?

_____

_____

37. Which of the following is *not* a catalyst element used in catalytic   37. _____
converters?

A. Palladium.

B. Platinum.

C. Rhodium.

D. Lead.

38. What is the primary purpose of an electronic control three-way catalytic conversion system?

_____

_____

_____

39. What is the theoretical air-fuel ratio maintained by the ECM?   39. _____

A. 14.5:1.

B. 14.9:1.

C. 14.7:1.

D. 15:1.

40. Describe the purpose of an exhaust gas analyzer.

_____

_____

41. Name some of the factors that affect an engine's ability to convert fuel into power.

_____

_____

42. Describe how an exhaust gas analyzer operates.

_____

_____

_____

_____

43. What type of engine problems can an exhaust gas analyzer diagnose?

_____

_____

_____

_____

Noise Control Systems

44. *True or False?* Many motorcycle exhaust systems, especially on
    street bikes, have one or more noise control feature built into
    them.

    44. _____

45. Name some of the acts that are considered as "tampering" with a motorcycle's noise control system.

    _____

    _____

    _____

    _____

    _____

    _____

Name _____

Date _____

Instructor _____

Period _____ Text pages 273-304

13

Power Transmission Systems

> **Objective:** After studying this chapter, you will be able to explain the basic operating principles, parts, and construction of a motorcycle's primary drive transmission and final drive assembly. Also, you will be able to describe the operation of electric starter/ignition systems and understand the operation and parts of chain, belt, and shaft final drives.
>
> **Instructions:** After studying the textbook, answer the workbook questions.

Primary Drive

1. Explain the function of a motorcycle's primary drive.

   _____

   _____

   _____

   _____

2. Primary drive reduction is accomplished by either a set of _____ or a(n) _____ and sprocket set.

   2. _____

3. Which of the following are gear designs used for primary gear drives?

   A. Straight-cut gears.

   B. Straight-cut offset gears.

   C. Helical gears.

   D. All of the above.

   3. _____

4. Identify this type of primary gear drive.

_____

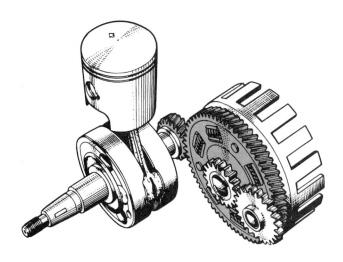

5. List the components that are part of a typical primary chain drive system.

_____

_____

_____

_____

6. A primary belt drive system is often used with a(n) _____ clutch in   6. _____
ATVs.

Clutches

7. Most motorcycle clutches are placed between the _____ and the   7. _____
_ _____.

8. List the two types of clutch actuation.

_____

_____

_____

_____

Name _____

9. Label the names of the parts of this manual multi-plate clutch.

A. _____

B. _____

C. _____

D. _____

E. _____

F. _____

G. _____

H. _____

I. _____

J. _____

10. What are the advantages of a wet clutch?

_____

_____

_____

_____

11. What prevents oil from entering a dry clutch's basket?

_____

_____

_____

_____

12. Name the two types of springs used in motorcycle clutches.

_____

_____

13. Explain the purpose of motorcycle clutch springs.

_____

_____

14. Describe the functions of a clutch shock absorber.

_____

_____

_____

_____

15. Why are sprag clutches used in motorcycle electric starter motors?

_____

_____

_____

_____

Manual Transmissions

16. Name the two types of shafts commonly used in a motorcycle transmission.

_____

_____

17. What is the function of a countershaft sprocket?

_____

_____

18. In the constant mesh transmission, the power is transmitted through the _____ to the mainshaft.

18. _____

19. In order to change drive ratios, a sliding gear or sliding dog splined to the manual transmission shaft, must be _____.

19. _____

20. How many shifting forks does a manual transmission normally have?

20. _____

    A. 2.

    B. 3.

    C. 1.

    D. Both A & B.

Name _____

1. What is the function of a gear selector mechanism?

_____

_____

_____

_____

22. Describe the function of a transmission indexer.

_____

_____

_____

_____

23. Explain how a neutral indicator switch operates.

_____

_____

_____

24. List the three common methods used to locate a transmission's shift drums.

_____

_____

_____

25. Name the two types of shift stoppers.

_____

_____

26. Gear engagement in a modern motorcycle transmission is normally accomplished by the use of _____.

26. _____

27. In most cases, the direct drive transmission has the _____ and _____ located on the same side of the engine.

27. _____

28. What type of vehicles use a dual-range transmission?

_____

_____

_____

29. List the basic parts of a dual-range transmission.

_____

_____

_____

Automatic Transmissions

30. What is a centrifugal clutch/variable belt transmission?

_____

_____

_____

31. Explain the applications of a planetary gearshift.

_____

_____

_____

Final Drive Systems

32. Describe the function of a motorcycle's final drive system.

_____

_____

_____

33. Name the three motorcycle final drive designs.

_____

_____

_____

34. Define the term _master link._

_____

_____

_____

35. Why must a motorcycle chain be properly lubricated and cleaned?

_____

_____

_____

36. A(n) _____ final drive system does not require as much   36. _____
    maintenance as a(n) _____ drive system.

Name _____

37. Identify this type of final drive system.

_____

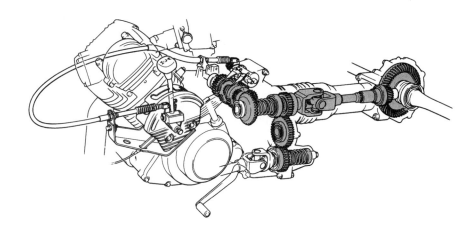

38. In a(n) _____ drive system, the final drive ratio refers to the number of teeth on the pinion gear versus the number of teeth on the ring gear.

38. _____

39. Drive ratio changes are accomplished by changing one or both chain or belt _____.

39. _____

40. Name some of the circumstances in which it may be necessary to change a motorcycle's final drive ratio.

_____

_____

_____

41. Define the term *overall ratio.*

_____

_____

_____

42. A touring motorcycle will normally have a(n) _____ ratio transmission.

42. _____

43. A motorcycle designed for motocross will normally have a(n) _____ ratio transmission.

43. _____

Starting Systems

44. Describe the purpose of a kickstart mechanism.

_____

_____

_____

45. Name three types of kickstart engagement devices.

_____

_____

46. _____ uses the primary drive's clutch outer hub for starting. 46. _____

47. What do non-primary kickstart mechanisms use to start the engine?

_____

48. Name the components in the following electric starter/ignition
system.

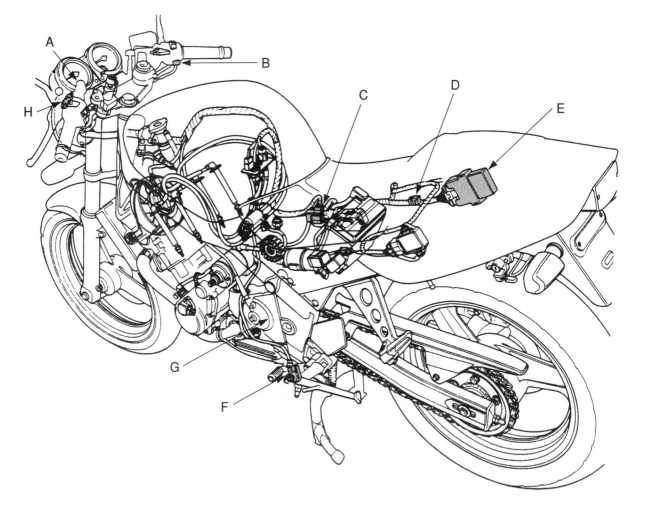

A. _____   E. _____

B. _____   F. _____

C. _____   G. _____

D. _____   H. _____

Name _____

49. The _____ detects the side stand position electrically.

49. _____

50. The operation of a motorcycle's starting system depends on the motorcycle's _____ and _____ system operation.

50. _____

51. *True or False?* A manual clutch motorcycle's starter motor will not operate unless the neutral switch is closed.

51. _____

52. To prevent vehicles with a centrifugal clutch from lurching forward when the engine starts, a(n) _____ prevents voltage from reaching the starter relay switch unless the brake is applied.

52. _____

53. *True or False?* CDI ignition systems with a side stand switch and/or neutral switch will not operate if the transmission is in gear.

53. _____

54. How does TPI systems integrated with a side stand and/or neutral switch control ignition?

_____

_____

55. A motorcycle is equipped with a transistorized ignition system, side stand switch, and neutral switch. The vehicle's side stand is up and the transmission is in first gear. Will this motorcycle's ignition system operate?

_____

_____

14

Wheels and Tires

Objective: After studying this chapter, you will be able to describe the types of tires and wheels used on modern motorcycles. Also, you will be able to perform service and repair operations on certain types of motorcycle tires and wheel assemblies.

Instructions: After studying the textbook, answer the workbook questions.

Wheels

1. A motorcycle wheel rotates on an axle and supports the _____.

1. _____

2. What does a motorcycle wire wheel consist of?

_____

_____

_____

3. A _____ wheel is manufactured by pouring molten metal into a mold.

3. _____

4. How is a stamped wheel held together?

_____

_____

_____

5. A(n) _____ passes through the motorcycle wheel's ball bearings and connects the wheel assembly to the rear swing arm or front fork legs.

5. _____

6. A motorcycle's rear wheel _____ provides a mounting place for the brake drum or brake disc and sprocket.

6. _____

Wheel Inspection

7. All the following are problems that can affect a motorcycle wheel's performance, EXCEPT:

   7. _____

   A. spokes can loosen or break.

   B. it could have static balance.

   C. rims get dented.

   D. may develop runout.

8. What procedure should be followed if abnormal conditions are suspected after inspecting a motorcycle's rear wheel for problems?

   _____

   _____

   _____

9. Explain what you should look for when inspecting a motorcycle wheel for problems.

   _____

   _____

   _____

   _____

   _____

   _____

Wheel Service

10. Describe the tasks that may be involved when servicing motorcycle wheels.

    _____

    _____

11. Why should you *not* use air pressure to spin wheel bearings while drying?

    _____

    _____

    _____

12. Name some of the problems to look for when inspecting a motorcycle wheel bearing.

    _____

    _____

    _____

Name _____

13. Describe the motorcycle wheel service procedure depicted in the illustration below.

_____

14. How can loose spokes damage a wheel?

_____

_____

15. Name the three methods used to check for loose wheel spokes.

_____

_____

_____

16. Which of the following is *not* part of the procedure for tightening   16. _____
    motorcycle wheel spokes?

   A. Spoke tightening should be done if only a small number of
      spokes are loose.

   B. If several spokes are loose, the wheel should be trued.

   C. Tighten all spokes on one side first.

   D. Let the air out of the tire after tightening the spokes.

17. What should be done if any wheel spoke requires more than two turns when tightening?

_____

_____

18. List the procedures to follow when replacing broken spokes.

_____

_____

19. Describe how to replace a dented wheel rim.

_____

_____

_____

_____

_____

Lacing and Truing a Wire Wheel Assembly

20. Define the term *wheel lacing.*

_____

_____

21. All the following require wheel lacing, EXCEPT: 21. _____

    A. spokes are loose.

    B. a new wheel is built from scratch.

    C. a hub is replaced.

    D. all spokes need replacement.

22. Identify the two types of wheel hubs.

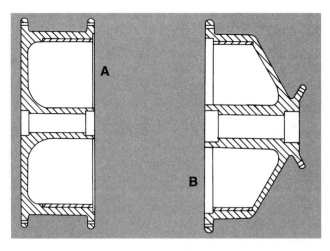

    A. _____

    B. _____

23. What is the major difference(s) in wheel spokes?   23. _____

    A. Length.

    B. Size of the spoke.

    C. Angle and length of the spoke throat.

    D. All of the above.

Name _____

24. The type of _____ and the intended use of the _____ determines   24. _____
    which type of spoke is used in the wheel.

25. Explain the term *spoke crossing pattern.*

    _____

    _____

26. Name two types of common spoke crossing patterns.

    _____

    _____

27. What is meant by the term *spoke angle?*

    _____

    _____

28. *True or False?* A rim intended for a symmetrical hub cannot be   28. _____
    properly laced to a conical hub.

29. All the following are steps in wheel lacing, EXCEPT: 29. _____

    A. screw nipples onto the spokes and tighten evenly.

    B. tighten spokes to true the wheel.

    C. select matching components and organize the spokes carefully.

    D. adjust lateral runout.

30. What does wheel truing involve?

    _____

    _____

31. _____ indicates how parallel the rim is to the hub.   31. _____

32. _____ shows how concentric the rim is with the hub.   32. _____

33. How is rim offset adjusted?

    _____

    _____

34. What rules should be remembered to make wheel truing easier?

    _____

    _____

    _____

    _____

35. When adjusting runout, it is best to get as close to _____ as   35. _____
    possible.

Tires

36. _____ use an air-filled tube within the tire's casing.

36. _____

37. _____ have a rubber layer glued to the inside that prevents air from filtering through.

37. _____

38. Which of the following is *not* an aspect to consider when replacing a motorcycle tire?

    A. Tire appearance.

    B. Tire construction.

    C. Size.

    D. Load and speed ratings.

38. _____

39. Name three types of motorcycle tires.

_____

_____

40. How is tire size determined?

_____

_____

41. Tire size markings are given on the tire _____.

41. _____

42. What does a tire size marking of 4.50H-17 indicate?

_____

_____

43. Describe what the letters appearing in the tire size markings represent.

_____

_____

44. What is indicated if a tire size marking contains the letter *V?*

_____

_____

45. Universal tires are considered to have dual designs suitable for both _____ and _____ use.

45. _____

46. What should you look for when inspecting the condition of a motorcycle tire?

_____

_____

47. _____ causes the tire's cord layers to separate and wear the sides of the tread.

47. _____

Name _____

48. _____ will cause the tire to skid and the tread to wear at its center.   48. _____

49. Explain how to remove a tire and disassemble it from the wheel of an ATV.

_____

_____

_____

_____

_____

_____

50. How should you break the bead on a tire if a bead breaker is *not* available?

_____

51. A(n) _____ makes tire replacement easier and helps   51. _____
prevent damage to cast and stamped wheels.

52. A _____ is a clamping device that pinches the tire beads against   52. _____
the rim.

53. Describe how to install a tubeless ATV tire on its rim.

_____

_____

_____

_____

_____

_____

_____

54. _____ tires can sometimes be repaired with a special plug   54. _____
patch kit.

55. Name two conditions which will change tire balance.

_____

_____

56. Describe how to balance a tire.

_____

_____

_____

_____

_____

_____

57. Explain the term *bubble balancer.*

_____

_____

_____

58. When storing a tire that is to be re-used, adjust air pressure to   58. _____
    _____ of the recommended pressure.

Troubleshooting Wheels and Tires

59. Which of the following would cause a motorcycle's front wheel to   59. _____
    wobble?

    A. Bent rim.

    B. Faulty tire.

    C. Worn front wheel bearing.

    D. All of the above.

60. A motorcycle's front wheel turns hard. Which of the following   60. _____
    would *not* cause this problem?

    A. Misadjusted brake.

    B. Misadjusted clutch cable.

    C. Faulty speedometer gear.

    D. Faulty wheel bearing

Name _____

Date _____

Instructor _____

Period _____ Text pages 327-352

15

Brakes

Objective: After studying this chapter, you will be able to explain the operating principles and construction of mechanical drum, hydraulic disc, ABS, and linked brake systems. Also, you will be able to describe how to troubleshoot and repair these systems.

Instructions: After studying the textbook, answer the workbook questions.

Brake Operation

1. What methods are used on motorcycles to apply the brakes?

   A. Hydraulic fluid.

   B. Cable.

   C. Mechanical linkage.

   D. All of the above.

1. _____

2. Name four essential motorcycle brake service and safety maintenance procedures.

   _____

   _____

   _____

3. What safety precautions should be taken when it is necessary to service a bike with asbestos pads?

   _____

   _____

   _____

4. Movement of the brake lever or pedal, is transferred to the brake actuating cam by a(n) _____ or _____.

4. _____

5. What determines the stopping ability of a mechanical brake system?

_____

_____

_____

6. In the hydraulic brake system, the lever or pedal uses _____ to   6. _____
   perform a mechanical function.

7. What are the advantages of using hydraulic brakes?

_____

_____

_____

8. All the following are basic parts of a hydraulic brake system,   8. _____
   EXCEPT:

   A. brake lever.

   B. cable.

   C. hydraulic lines.

   D. caliper and wheel cylinder.

9. Identify the parts of the following hydraulic brake system.

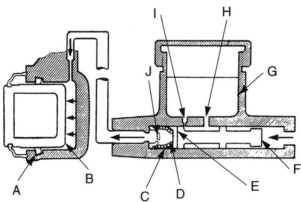

A. _____

B. _____

C. _____

D. _____

E. _____

F. _____

G. _____

H. _____

I. _____

J. _____

Name _____

10. Explain the operation of a hydraulic brake system's master cylinder.

_____
_____
_____
_____
_____
_____
_____
_____

Brake Design

11. Name the two basic drum brake designs used on motorcycles.

_____

12. The first shoe to act upon the drum is called the _____.

12. _____

13. Name the two types of calipers used on motorcycle hydraulic disc brakes.

_____

14. In a(n) _____ caliper, both pads press against the brake disc through a reaction of the sliding caliper yoke.

14. _____

15. A _____ caliper is rigidly mounted to the motorcycle's fork leg.

15. _____

16. Identify this type of caliper.

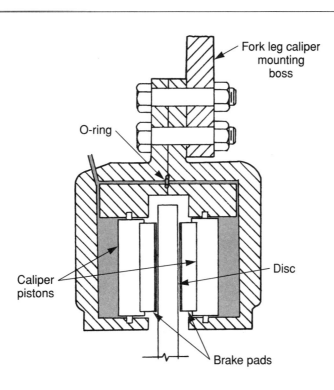

17. What type of motorcycle would normally use a *floating disc brake?*   17. _____

18. Why are brake discs commonly drilled or grooved?

_____

_____

19. List the three types of brake fluid.

_____

_____

20. The _____ designations specify the brake fluid's ability to   20. _____
withstand heat without boiling.

21. Why is it important *not* to mix incompatible brake fluids?

_____

_____

Brake Inspection, Maintenance, and Repair

22. When removing a motorcycle's front wheel, support the bike   22. _____
securely under the _____ to raise the wheel.

23. Describe the proper methods used to remove a motorcycle's front wheel.

_____

_____

_____

_____

_____

24. Explain how to install a motorcycle's front wheel equipped with hydraulic disc brakes.

_____

_____

_____

_____

_____

25. Name the three operations of brake service.

_____

_____

Name _____

26. Relining drum brakes involves the replacement of the _____.   26. _____

27. List the steps to follow when replacing worn or defective shoes on drum brakes.

_____

_____

_____

_____

_____

_____

_____

28. What procedures should be followed when inspecting a hydraulic brake system?

_____

_____

_____

_____

_____

29. What is the purpose of *bleeding* hydraulic brakes?

_____

30. When should you bleed a motorcycle brake system?

_____

_____

31. Which of the following is *not* a rule to remember when rebuilding   31. _____
    a master cylinder?

    A. Discard all old brake fluid.

    B. Do not allow oil, grease, or brake fluid to come into contact
       with the brake disc or pads.

    C. Always bleed the system after reassembly.

    D. Use parts solvent for cleaning parts exposed to brake fluid.

32. Which of the following is one of the procedures to follow during a   32. _____
    typical disc brake caliper rebuild?

    A. Clean the pads with brake fluid.

    B. Use a micrometer to measure the caliper piston diameter.

    C. Lubricate the rotor linings with approved DOT fluid.

    D. Reuse the old rubber parts.

Unified Brake Controls

33. Rear brakes only give about _____ of maximum stopping power.   33. _____

Linked Braking System (LBS)

34. Explain the term *linked braking system.*

_____

_____

35. Identify the basic parts of the motorcycle linked braking system.

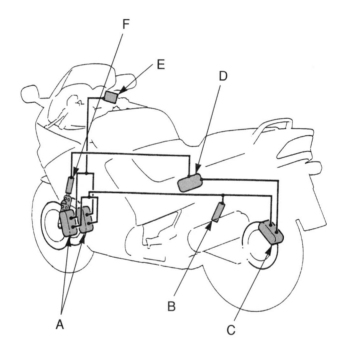

A. _____

B. _____

C. _____

D. _____

E. _____

F. _____

Name _____

36. Describe the operation of a linked braking system.

_____
_____
_____
_____
_____
_____
_____
_____
_____
_____
_____
_____
_____
_____

37. What is the *heart* of a motorcycle linked braking system?

_____
_____
_____
_____

Anti-lock Brake Systems (ABS)

38. Describe the function of a motorcycle anti-lock brake system.

_____
_____
_____
_____

39. What controls the front and rear brake systems on a motorcycle anti-lock brake system?

_____
_____
_____
_____

40. Label the names of the components of this anti-lock brake system.

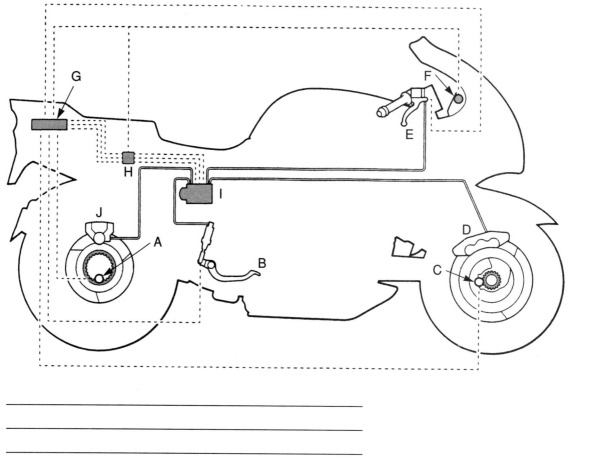

A. _____

B. _____

C. _____

D. _____

E. _____

F. _____

G. _____

H. _____

I. _____

J. _____

41. _____ current is generated by an anti-lock brake system wheel sensor when the wheel rotates.

41. _____

42. In a typical ABS motorcycle, the sensor rotor on the front wheel has _____.

42. _____

Name _____

43. Describe the operation of a motorcycle anti-lock brake system's electronic control module.

_____

_____

_____

_____

_____

_____

44. The functions performed by the anti-lock brake ECM consists of   44. _____
_____ and _____.

45. The _____ is a component that controls the anti-lock brake   45. _____
system's hydraulic pressure, based on instructions from the ECM.

46. Describe the function of an anti-lock brake system's fail safe relay.

_____

_____

47. The _____ informs the rider of the ABS self-diagnosis results.   47. _____

48. What happens if an anti-lock brake system's ECM detects a fault in the system?

_____

_____

_____

49. Briefly describe the operation of a motorcycle anti-lock brake system.

_____

_____

_____

_____

_____

_____

_____

_____

50. With motorcycles equipped with anti-lock brakes, sudden _____   50. _____
while cornering is not recommended.

Troubleshooting Motorcycle Brake Systems

51. A motorcycle equipped with drum brakes has poor brake performance. Which of the following would cause this condition?

    A. Worn brake cam.

    B. Worn brake linings.

    C. Worn brake shoes at cam contact areas.

    D. All of the above.

51. _____

52. A motorcycle equipped with drum brakes is brought into the shop. The owner complains that the brake lever returns too slowly. What are the possible causes of this problem?

    A. Worn brake cam.

    B. Contaminated brake linings

    C. Leaking wheel cylinder.

    D. Worn brake linings

52. _____

53. What would cause motorcycle drum brakes to squeak?

    A. Worn caliper piston.

    B. Worn brake pad.

    C. Worn brake drum.

    D. None of the above.

53. _____

54. Which of the following would *not* cause brake fluid leakage in a motorcycle hydraulic disc brake system?

    A. Insufficient tightening of connection points.

    B. Cracked hose.

    C. Clogged brake hose.

    D. Worn wheel cylinder piston.

54. _____

55. The ABS warning light comes on only when the motorcycle is moving. Which of the following would cause this condition?

    A. Defective ECM.

    B. Defective wheel speed sensor.

    C. Excessive clearance between wheel sensor and solenoid.

    D. Both A and B.

55. _____

16

Frame and Suspension Systems

Objective: After studying this chapter, you will be able to identify different types of modern motorcycle main frames. Also, you will be able to explain basic troubleshooting, service, and repair procedures for today's motorcycle frames and suspension systems.

Instructions: After studying the textbook, answer the workbook questions.

Frame

1. Which of the following describes the function of a motorcycle frame?

   A. Provide a non-flexing mount for the engine, suspension, and wheels.

   B. Provides a rigid structure between the steering head and rear swingarm.

   C. Adds weight to the bike.

   D. Both A & B.

   1. _____

2. The material used for a frame is chosen to match the motorcycle's _____.

   2. _____

3. _____ frames are reserved exclusively for on-road sport bikes with medium-to-large displacement engines.

   3. _____

4. Name two materials used to make motorcycle frames.

   _____

5. What are the advantages of using titanium alloys on certain motorcycle chassis sub-frames?

   _____

   _____

6. When maximum strength is required in a vertical direction and   6. _____
strength in a horizontal direction is not as important, _____ tubing
is used as part of the motorcycle's frame.

7. In order to prevent excessive vibration to the rider and premature   7. _____
fatigue to structural members, the motorcycle frame is chosen
according to _____ and by the specific use of the machine.

8. Identify the parts of the following single cradle frame.

A. _____

B. _____

C. _____

9. What type of motorcycles normally use a double cradle frame?

_____

10. Describe the construction of a double cradle frame.

_____

_____

11. In the backbone frame, the _____ hangs from the top of the frame   11. _____
and acts as a structural member.

12. Explain the term *stamped frame.*

_____

_____

13. What type of motorcycles use stamped frames?

_____

14. The chassis of most ATVs are made of _____ and ruggedly   14. _____
constructed.

    A. plastic

    B. steel

    C. aluminum

    D. fiberglass

Name _____

15. What type of metal is scooter frames normally made of?

_____

_____

Frame Inspection

16. Explain what should be done if a motorcycle's rear wheel leans to either side when viewed from above.

_____

_____

Front Suspension

17. Describe the purpose of a motorcycle suspension system.

_____

_____

18. Explain the term *telescopic front suspension.*

_____

_____

19. _____ provide a mounting place for the front wheel axle on a   19. _____
    telescoping fork assembly.

20. What keeps oil from leaking out of a telescoping fork assembly?

_____

21. List the two phases of telescoping fork operation.

_____

_____

22. Suspension adjustment is accomplished on a telescopic front   22. _____
    suspension system by all the following methods, EXCEPT:

    A. changing oil viscosity.

    B. changing spring rates.

    C. adjusting damping valves.

    D. changing fork oil.

23. An anti-dive fork front suspension design normally uses _____   23. _____
    pressure to help prevent front end dive during braking.

24. Describe the construction of a pivoting link front suspension system.

_____

_____

_____

_____

_____

25. What is the primary function of a pivoting link front suspension system oil damper?

_____

_____

26. Name the two categories of pivoting link front suspension.

_____

_____

_____

_____

27. The single-sided swingarm front suspension is used only with a so-called _____ frame.

27. _____

28. Identify this type of front suspension.

_____

Name _____

29. Define the term *steering geometry*.

_____

_____

_____

30. Which of the following are factors that determine steering   30. _____
    geometry?

    A. Rake.

    B. Trail.

    C. Offset.

    D. All of the above.

31. _____ is the angle of the forks from true vertical.   31. _____

32. _____ is the distance along the ground between a line down   32. _____
    the centerline of the forks and a vertical line through the axle
    centerline.

33. _____ provides the proper steering arc.   33. _____

34. Define the term *steering damper.*

_____

_____

_____

35. What operations are part of typical motorcycle front suspension service?

_____

_____

_____

36. What determines the frequency of fork oil changing?   36. _____

    A. Riding conditions.

    B. Manufacturer recommendations.

    C. Quality of fork oil.

    D. Both A & B.

37. How often should the fork oil be changed even under the most ideal conditions?

_____

_____

_____

38. _____ bearings are the most common type of steering head   38. _____
    bearings.

39. _____ bearings used as steering head bearings have the advantage   39. _____
    of extremely long service life and ease of assembly and
    disassembly.

40. The most frequent reason for fork disassembly is _____.   40. _____

41. What does a motorcycle fork rebuild involve?

    _____

    _____

42. What rules should be remembered when servicing a motorcycle fork?

    _____

    _____

    _____

    _____

    _____

Rear Suspension Systems

43. A typical motorcycle rear suspension consists of a(n) _____ and   43. _____
    one or more _____.

44. Which of the following is *not* used to attach a rear suspension   44. _____
    swingarm to the motorcycle frame?

    A. Weld joint.

    B. Pivot bolt.

    C. Shaft.

    D. Link.

45. What materials are used to manufacture motorcycle swingarms?

    _____

    _____

    _____

46. Balancing a motorcycle's suspension properly from _____ to   46. _____
    _____ is the most critical adjustment for a good ride and
    performance.

47. Describe how to check a motorcycle's suspension balance.

    _____

    _____

    _____

48. Rear shock absorbers work much like a front suspension _____.   48. _____

Name _____

49. Identify the parts of the following oil damped rear shock absorber.

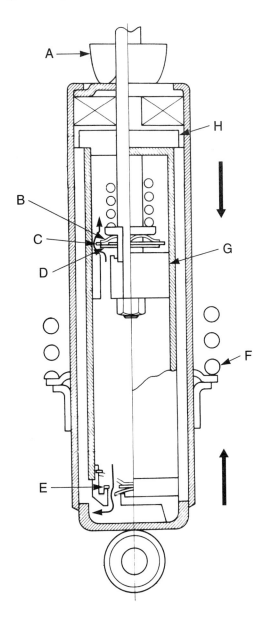

A. _____

B. _____

C. _____

D. _____

E. _____

F. _____

G. _____

H. _____

50. What type of motorcycle would use large capacity gas-oil shocks?

    A. Cruising bikes.

    B. Touring bikes.

    C. Off-road bikes.

    D. Standard.

50. _____

51. Name three types of motorcycle shock absorber springs.

_____

_____

_____

52. Shock absorbers are bolted to the frame and swingarm through _____ or _____.

52. _____

53. Explain the function of a motorcycle side stand.

_____

_____

_____

Frame and Suspension Inspection

54. List the areas to check when inspecting a motorcycle's mid-frame.

_____

_____

_____

_____

_____

55. Define the term *toe-in*.

_____

_____

_____

56. _____ is the inward or outward tilt of the wheel at the top.

56. _____

57. Define the term *caster*.

_____

_____

_____

Name _____

8. Describe how to check for a toe-in condition on an ATV four wheel vehicle.

_____

_____

_____

_____

_____

_____

_____

9. Identify the procedure shown here. Also, identify the equipment
used in this operation.

_____

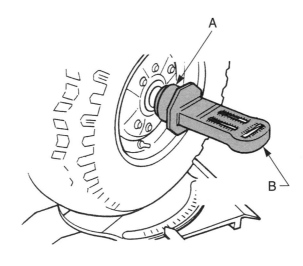

A. _____

B. _____

Frame Problems

60. A motorcycle has an abnormal engine vibration problem. Which of
the following would cause this condition?

    A. Bent or damaged frame.

    B. Damaged fork.

    C. Cracked or damaged engine mounts.

    D. Both A & B.

60. _____

61. A motorcycle steers to one side during acceleration. Which of the following is the possible cause of this problem?

    A. Bent or damaged frame.

    B. Bent wheel rim.

    C. Bent fork.

    D. Bent swingarm.

61. _____

Front Suspension Problems

62. A motorcycle is brought into the shop with a hard steering problem. What could be the cause of this problem?

    A. Faulty steering head bearing.

    B. Faulty tire.

    C. Insufficient tire pressure.

    D. All of the above.

62. _____

63. Which of the following would cause a motorcycle to steer to one side?

    A. Incorrect shock adjustment.

    B. Bent fork.

    C. Faulty shock spring.

    D. All of the above.

63. _____

64. A motorcycle has a soft suspension problem. Name some of the possible causes of this condition.

_____

_____

_____

_____

65. What would cause a motorcycle to have a hard suspension problem?

_____

_____

_____

_____

66. Lack of grease in the speedometer _____ would produce a noisy front suspension problem in a motorcycle.

66. _____

Name _____

Rear Suspension Problems

67. List the causes of rear wheel wobble on a motorcycle.

_____

_____

_____

_____

68. _____ springs would cause a soft rear suspension problem on a motorcycle.

68. _____

69. *True or False?* A bent swingarm pivot can produce a hard rear suspension problem on a motorcycle.

69. _____

70. What would cause a motorcycle to have a noisy rear suspension?

_____

_____

_____

17

Accessory Systems

Objective: After studying this chapter, you will be able to describe the construction, operation, and certain troubleshooting procedures for a motorcycle lighting system and other accessory devices.

Instructions: After studying the textbook, answer the workbook questions.

Accessory Systems

1. What circuits are part of a motorcycle's accessory system?

_____

_____

_____

_____

Lighting Systems

2. Which of the following are types of motorcycle lighting systems?

   A. Dc lighting that is powered by the battery.

   B. Ac lighting that receives power from the alternator coil.

   C. Dc lighting from a solar panel.

   D. Both A & B.

2. _____

3. On _____ motorcycle lighting systems, the headlight comes on when the engine starts.

3. _____

4. Identify the components of the following motorcycle lighting system.

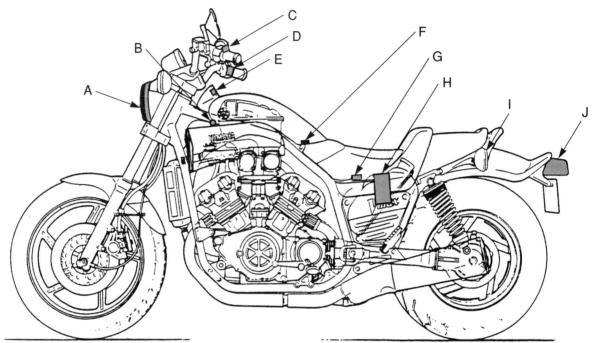

A. _____

B. _____

C. _____

D. _____

E. _____

F. _____

G. _____

H. _____

I. _____

J. _____

5. What is the most common headlight bulb used on modern motorcycles?

_____

6. When making a headlight adjustment, make sure the _____ pressure is correct and the _____ is approximately half full.

6. _____

7. A motorcycle headlight is switched from high beam to low beam by the use of a(n) _____.

7. _____

8. Most state laws require that tail lights on street vehicles be _____ powered so they will remain on, even if the engine stalls.

8. _____

Name _____

9. When a motorcycle's brake light and tail light are a combined unit, _____ filaments are usually employed.

9. _____

10. What lights are part of the turn signal indicator light circuit?

_____

_____

11. How does a motorcycle turn signal flasher operate?

_____

_____

_____

_____

12. Name the two types of motorcycle instrument panel displays.

_____

_____

Lighting System Problems

13. What instruments are usually needed when troubleshooting motorcycle lighting system problems?

_____

_____

14. Which of the following is *not* part of the procedure to troubleshoot lighting system problems?

14. _____

A. Check for voltage in the circuit.

B. Replace lights until the defect is found.

C. Check the continuity of switches and wiring.

D. Verify the circuit has a good ground.

15. The logical place to start troubleshooting motorcycle lighting system problems is at the _____.

15. _____

16. How can loose or corroded connections affect the operation of a motorcycle's electrical system?

_____

_____

17. Corrosive electrical contacts can be repaired by using _____ on the affected areas.

17. _____

18. What normally causes *flickering lights* in a motorcycle lighting system?

_____

_____

19. How should you check a motorcycle's brake light switch operation and adjustment?

_____

_____

_____

20. When should a motorcycle's rear brake light come on?

_____

_____

_____

21. Explain how to adjust a motorcycle's rear brake light switch.

_____

_____

_____

_____

22. What should be checked for *first* if a motorcycle's brake light fails   22. _____
    to come on?

    A. Dead battery.

    B. Pinched or chaffed wire.

    C. Burned out bulb.

    D. Poor ground.

23. Describe the lighting system troubleshooting procedure depicted in the following illustration.

_____

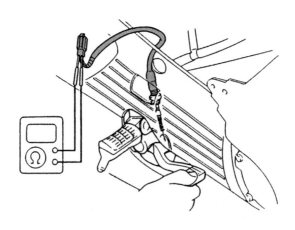

Name _____

24. What should you look for if a motorcycle's turn signal light does *not* blink?

_____

_____

_____

_____

Warning and Indicator Circuits

25. Explain how a four-stroke motorcycle engine's oil pressure warning light operates.

_____

_____

26. What procedures should be followed if a four-stroke motorcycle engine's oil pressure warning light does not come on with the ignition switch turned on?

_____

_____

_____

27. Describe the operation of a liquid-cooled motorcycle engine's coolant temperature gauge.

_____

_____

_____

_____

_____

_____

28. Explain how a motorcycle fuel level gauge operates.

_____

_____

_____

_____

29. Which of the following are types of motorcycle fuel gauges?   29. _____

   A. Return-type.

   B. Stop-type.

   C. Bulb-type.

   D. Both A & B.

30. Describe how a low fuel indicator operates.

_____

_____

_____

_____

_____

_____

_____

31. A motorcycle's brake fluid warning light is connected to the brake   31. _____
fluid level sensor in the _____.

32. Explain the operation of a brake fluid warning light.

_____

_____

_____

33. What type of charging gauges are used on most motorcycle charging systems?

_____

_____

34. A(n) _____ charging gauge is placed in series with the   34. _____
motorcycle's battery and alternator.

35. Which of the following is *true* about a check engine light?

A. This warning light indicates the condition of the vehicle's electronic control systems.

B. The light may come on while the engine is running.

C. The check engine light may be triggered by the engine control computer.

D. All of the above.

36. Certain types of motorcycles which use a(n) _____ are normally   36. _____
equipped with a sidestand indicator light.

37. What is the function of an anti-lock brake light?

_____

38. Explain the operation of an electronic speedometer.

_____

_____

_____

_____

_____

Name _____

39. How does a motorcycle's tachometer operate?

_____

_____

_____

_____

Switches

40. Switches can be tested for continuity with a(n) _____ or a(n)   40. _____
_____ at the switch connector plug by operating positions and
comparing results with the switch operation.

41. A motorcycle horn circuit consists of what parts?

_____

_____

42. Describe the procedures to follow when a motorcycle's horn doesn't work.

_____

_____

_____

_____

_____

Communication Systems

43. Name some of the communication systems available on modern
cruiser and touring motorcycles.

_____

_____

_____

_____

44. List the most common areas of problems found in modern motorcycle communication systems.

_____

_____

_____

45. What should be checked first if a motorcycle's AM/FM radio system is not working?

_____

_____

Cruise Control

46. Explain the function of a motorcycle's cruise control system.

_____

_____

47. What type of motorcycles are normally equipped with an electronic cruise control system?

_____

48. List the basic components of a motorcycle's cruise control system.

_____

_____

49. Describe how a cruise control system works.

_____

_____

_____

_____

_____

50. Name some of the methods used to cancel cruise control operation.

_____

_____

_____

_____

_____

_____

18

Engine and Power Transmission Disassembly

Objective: After studying this chapter, you will be able to perform the proper procedures required to remove and disassemble a modern motorcycle engine, its primary drive, transmission, and final drive. Also, you will discover how heat and special holding and pulling devices aid in the removal and disassembly of motorcycle engines and drive train components.

Instructions: After studying the textbook, answer the workbook questions.

Preparing for Engine Removal

1. Why is proper work area organization essential during motorcycle engine teardown?

_____

_____

_____

_____

2. What should be the *first* step performed before removing a motorcycle engine from its frame?

_____

_____

_____

3. All the following service procedures require motorcycle engine removal, EXCEPT:

    A. top-end overhaul.

    B. spark plug replacement.

    C. transmission repair.

    D. complete engine overhaul.

3. _____

4. Which of the following is provided in a motorcycle service manual?

   4. _____

   A. Which way the engine comes out of the frame.

   B. The location of engine mounting bolts.

   C. Which cables, linkages, and electrical wires must be disconnected.

   D. All of the above.

Drain Fluids

5. Why is it important to inspect the oil filter for debris after draining the motorcycle's engine oil?

   _____

   _____

   _____

6. What is indicated if a motorcycle's engine oil is milky in appearance?

   _____

   _____

7. When removing a two-stroke motorcycle engine equipped with oil injection, always remember to disconnect and plug the _____.

   7. _____

Disconnect Electrical System

8. Why should you always remove the motorcycle's battery during engine removal?

   _____

   _____

   _____

9. Describe how to properly remove a motorcycle's battery.

   _____

   _____

   _____

   _____

Name _____

10. Identify the common types of connectors used in a motorcycle electrical system.

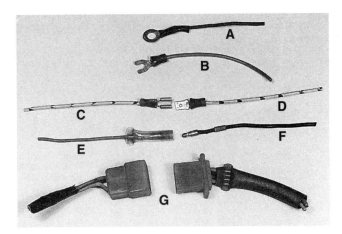

A. _____

B. _____

C. _____

D. _____

E. _____

F. _____

G. _____

Disconnect Control Cables

11. List some of the cables which may require disconnection during motorcycle engine removal.

_____

_____

_____

_____

12. Why should you mark the function of each cable?

_____

Fuel System Disassembly

13. Why should you remove the motorcycle's carburetor(s) before engine removal?

_____

_____

14. All the following is(are) used to attach the carburetor(s)   14. _____
    to the motorcycle engine, EXCEPT:

    A. sleeve.

    B. spigot.

    C. tube.

    D. flange.

15. After removing the carburetor(s) from the motorcycle's engine, why is it important to drain the fuel from the float bowls and store the carburetor(s) properly?

    _____

    _____

16. On an EFI motorcycle engine, why should the injectors be marked if they are removed?

    _____

    _____

Disconnect Final Drive

17. Which of the following should *not* be done to a motorcycle chain   17. _____
    prior to engine removal?

    A. The chain should be cleaned.

    B. Inspect the chain.

    C. Lubricant should be applied to the chain before storage.

    D. All lubricant should be removed from the chain before storage.

Removing Engine from Motorcycle

18. Name some of the precautions that should be taken before removing a motorcycle engine from the frame.

    _____

    _____

    _____

    _____

19. List the safety rules to follow during motorcycle engine removal.

    _____

    _____

    _____

Name _____

20. Identify this piece of equipment used during motorcycle engine rebuilding.

_____

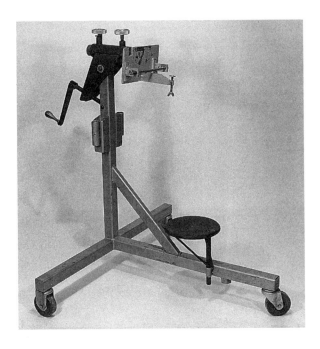

21. Why is it important to orderly store parts and bolts during motorcycle engine removal?

_____

_____

_____

_____

22. When disassembling an engine for the first time, you should place   22. _____
    _____ or _____ on parts to aid reassembly.

23. Name two methods commonly used during engine removal to keep motorcycle engine fastener location prop-
    erly organized.

_____

_____

_____

_____

24. _____ and _____ are used to properly locate, align, or provide   24. _____
    clearance for certain engine parts.

Dividing the Engine

25. Identify the five groups of the following motorcycle engine.

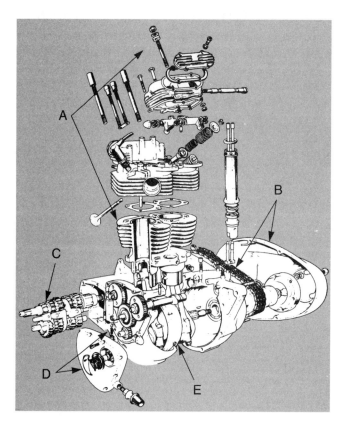

A. _____

B. _____

C. _____

D. _____

E. _____

26. The _____ of a motorcycle engine consists of the parts from the cylinder base up.

26. _____

27. The _____ of a motorcycle engine is the group of components contained within the crankcase, excluding the transmission.

27. _____

28. List some of the parts that make up the right and left side of a motorcycle engine.

_____

_____

_____

_____

_____

Name _____

29. Removal of left and right side parts allow access to the motorcycle engine's _____.

29. _____

30. On horizontally opposed or transverse V-type motorcycle engines, the left and right sides are called _____ and _____.

30. _____

31. What parts are part of the engine/transmission division of a motorcycle engine?

31. _____

32. Most motorcycles use a(n) _____ type transmission division.

32. _____

Holders and Pullers

33. Define the term *engine holder.*

_____

_____

_____

_____

34. Define the term *puller.*

_____

_____

_____

_____

35. List five of the most common engine holders.

_____

_____

_____

_____

_____

36. Name some of the motorcycle components which may require the use of a puller.

_____

_____

_____

_____

Using Heat to Aid Disassembly

37. Heating a part causes it to _____.

37. _____

38. Which of the following is *not* an acceptable method of heating parts?

38. _____

    A. Furnace.

    B. Hot plate.

    C. Propane torch.

    D. Oven.

39. Describe some of the rules to follow when using heat to aid motorcycle part removal.

_____

_____

_____

_____

_____

_____

Sequence of Disassembly

40. What determines the sequence of motorcycle engine disassembly?

_____

_____

41. Which of the following are common problems you may encounter when removing the wrist pin from a motorcycle's piston?

41. _____

    A. Varnish formed on wrist pin.

    B. Peened edge (burred edge) next to wrist pin circlip.

    C. Tightly bonded gasket.

    D. Both A & B.

42. What type of problems can occur when disassembling a motorcycle engine's cylinder head?

_____

_____

43. Describe the problems that may be encountered when removing a motorcycle engine's flywheel.

_____

_____

Name _____

44. What difficulties may be encountered when attempting to separate a motorcycle engine's crankcase?

_____

_____

_____

_____

45. Identify this motorcycle engine disassembly procedure.

_____

Name _____

Date _____

Instructor _____

Period _____ Text pages 409-430

19

Two-Stroke Engine Overhaul

Objective: After studying this chapter, you will be able to disassemble, recondition, and assemble a motorcycle two-stroke engine. Also, you will learn how to troubleshoot common two-stroke engine problems and install a two-stroke engine in a motorcycle frame.

Instructions: After studying the textbook, answer the workbook questions.

Engine Top End Service

1. What part(s) are *not* included in a two-stroke motorcycle engine's top end?

    A. Cylinder head.

    B. Crankshaft.

    C. Cylinder.

    D. Reed valve.

1. _____

2. Why does a two-stroke engine's top end require more frequent service and repair than a four-stroke engine?

_____

_____

_____

Cylinder and Piston Inspection

3. Describe what to look for when checking a motorcycle engine cylinder for problems.

_____

_____

4. All the following are methods used to check a motorcycle engine   4. _____
   cylinder for cracks, EXCEPT:

   A. powder tests.

   B. pressure checking.

   C. magnetic detection.

   D. magnetic resonance imaging.

5. A ridge or lip at the top and/or bottom of the engine cylinder is   5. _____
   due to _____.

6. Explain the causes of cylinder scoring.

   _____

   _____

7. Piston galling can be caused by _____ and _____.   7. _____

8. Name the conditions that can be determined by piston and cylinder measurements.

   _____

   _____

   _____

   _____

   _____

9. Piston skirt wear is checked by measuring the piston skirt diameter   9. _____
   with a(n) _____.

10. How is ring land wear determined?

    _____

    _____

11. Explain how to check piston ring fit.

    _____

    _____

12. Measurement of piston _____ indicates the ring size.   12. _____

13. Measurement of the _____ indicates the amount of ring tension.   13. _____

14. Define the term *cylinder taper*.

    _____

    _____

15. What type of engine problems are produced by cylinder taper?

    _____

    _____

Name _____

16. How is piston-to-cylinder clearance determined?

_____

_____

Engine Decarbonizing

17. How can excessive carbon buildup in a two-stroke engine's top end affect engine performance?

_____

_____

_____

18. Identify the part cleaning machine depicted in the following illustration.

_____

Parts Reconditioning and Replacement

19. List the steps to follow to deglaze an engine cylinder.

_____

_____

_____

_____

_____

20. Why should you be careful not to pull the spinning hone completely out of the cylinder during deglazing?

_____

_____

_____

21. If an engine cylinder is within wear limits, but the piston is worn   21. _____
    undersize, a new _____ and _____ should be installed.

22. Describe the function of cylinder boring.

_____

_____

_____

23. Motorcycle engine cylinders which use a(n) _____ sleeve must be   23. _____
    replaced after the largest overbore has been used.

24. What is the purpose of honing a cylinder after it has been bored?

_____

_____

_____

Engine Lower End Service

25. Which of the following is *not* a part of the inspection and service   25. _____
    of a two-stroke cycle engine lower end?

    A. Honing the cylinder.

    B. Measuring connecting rod bearing clearance.

    C. Checking main bearing condition.

    D. Reconditioning and truing the crankshaft.

26. Name two procedures used for measuring connecting rod bearing clearance.

_____

_____

_____

27. The rod bearing and crankshaft must be free of _____ for accurate   27. _____
    measurement of connecting rod play.

Name _____

28. Identify the following motorcycle engine lower end service
   procedure.

28. _____

29. What should be done if rod side play or big end bearing clearance does not meet service manual specifications?

_____

_____

30. Main bearings should be checked for _____ and _____ play.   30. _____

31. Why shouldn't you spin bearings with compressed air when drying?

_____

_____

32. If main bearing lateral and radial play is within service limits,
   visually inspect the _____ for evidence of pitting, chipping,
   discoloration, or signs of overheating.

32. _____

   A. balls

   B. races

   C. cages

   D. All of the above.

33. What does motorcycle engine crankshaft reconditioning involve?

_____

_____

34. Name some of the special tools and equipment required during crankshaft reconditioning.

_____

_____

35. Explain *crankshaft disassembly?*

_____

_____

36. Why should you be careful when using a press to disassemble or reassemble a crankshaft?

_____

_____

37. Define the term *crankshaft truing.*

_____

_____

38. A crankshaft truing stand is used to determine and measure _____.

Engine Diagnosis

39. Motorcycle engine normal wear is easily diagnosed during _____   39. _____
    disassembly and measurement.

40. What is the cause of engine blowby?

_____

_____

41. Name three serious engine problems that are the result of blowby.

_____

_____

42. List some of the causes of two-stroke engine lubrication failures.

_____

_____

43. All the following are common foreign materials found in a   43. _____
    two-stroke engine, EXCEPT:

    A. dirt.

    B. sand.

    C. mixed fuel and oil.

    D. mud.

44. Name some of the two-stroke engine problems caused by foreign materials.

_____

_____

Name _____

45. List four causes of two-stroke engine overheating.

_____

_____

_____

_____

46. What is two-stroke engine ignition related overheating normally caused by?

_____

_____

47. Describe the two most common causes for two-stroke engine detonation.

_____

_____

48. Preignition occurs when a(n) _____ in the combustion chamber   48. _____
    ignites the air-fuel mixture before the spark plug fires.

49. Name some of the causes of fuel system overheating.

_____

_____

_____

_____

50. Explain two methods used to measure crankshaft and transmission shaft end play.

_____

_____

_____

_____

Engine Reassembly

51. The most critical motorcycle engine seals are those which seal the   51. _____
    _____ and _____.

52. What rules should be remembered when installing motorcycle engine lip seals?

_____

_____

_____

53. During engine assembly, two-stroke engine components should be   53. _____
    lubricated with _____.

54. Grease can be used on which of the following parts during two-stroke engine assembly?

54. _____

    A. Seals.

    B. On rollers during crankshaft assembly.

    C. Shims.

    D. All of the above.

Top End Reassembly

55. Identify the following two-stroke engine reassembly procedure.

_____

56. A(n) _____ follows a crisscross pattern from the center to the outside of the part.

56. _____

57. What is the purpose of a two-stroke engine crankcase leak test?

— _____

— _____

58. List in order the four steps to follow to perform a two-stroke engine crankcase leak test.

_____

_____

_____

_____

Name _____

Installing Engine in Frame

59. What are the first steps that should be performed before attempting to install the motorcycle engine in the frame?

_____

_____

_____

60. List the procedures to follow after a motorcycle engine has been reinstalled in its frame.

_____

_____

_____

_____

_____

_____

Initial Engine Start-Up and Operation

61. Why is it important to follow break-in procedures after a motorcycle engine has been overhauled?

_____

62. After a motorcycle engine has been overhauled, the typical break-in period is _____ hours for an off-road bike and _____ miles for a road motorcycle.

62. _____

63. *True or False?* Should the fuel tank be filled with oil before engine start-up if premix lubrication is used?

63. _____

64. What procedures should be followed before attempting to start a freshly overhauled two-stroke motorcycle engine?

_____

_____

_____

_____

_____

65. List the steps to follow after an overhauled two-stroke motorcycle engine has been started.

_____

_____

_____

_____

20

Four-Stroke Engine Overhaul

Objective: After studying this chapter, you will be able to perform a complete overhaul on a four-stroke motor-cycle engine. You will also be able to install a four-stroke engine in its frame and explain basic initial starting and engine break-in procedures.

Instructions: After studying the textbook, answer the workbook questions.

Engine Top End Service

1. What are the functions of a motorcycle engine top end?

_____

_____

_____

_____

2. Which of the following is *not* a part of a four-stroke motorcycle   2. _____
   engine valve train?

   A. Piston pin and connecting rod.

   B. Camshaft and bearings.

   C. Push rods and lifters.

   D. Valve seats and faces.

3. What should you look for when inspecting the condition of a four-stroke engine's camshaft and bearings?

_____

_____

_____

4. Describe the four-stroke engine valve train service procedure depicted in the following illustration.

_____

_____

5. The simplest way to measure cam lobes for wear is to use a(n) _____.

5. _____

6. In push rod engines, the camshaft or camshafts are located in the _____.

6. _____

7. What is the first thing you should do when removing cam followers and rocker arms for inspection?

_____

_____

8. If a cam follower is scuffed or dished, it must be _____.

8. _____

9. What is the location(s) cam followers and rocker arms normally wear?

9. _____

   A. At the valve end.

   B. At the camshaft end (follower) or push rod end (rocker).

   C. Where the rocker shaft passes through the follower or rocker.

   D. All of the above.

10. What should an inspection of cam followers, rocker arms, and shaft include?

_____

_____

11. In push rod motorcycle engines, the lifters may be located in the _____ or in the _____.

11. _____

12. Where are the camshaft(s) always located in a push rod engine?

_____

_____

Name _____

13. What should you look for when inspecting push rods and lifters?

_____

_____

14. The most common method of driving a four-stroke motorcycle   14. _____
engine's camshaft is with a(n) _____ and _____.

15. Most motorcycle four-stroke engine's _____ cams require a   15. _____
tensioner and one or more guides.

16. Identify the following type of motorcycle engine camshaft drive.

_____

17. Why should you use care when cleaning four-stroke engine valve springs?

_____

_____

18. What should you look for when performing a four-stroke valve   18. _____
spring inspection?

A. Rust or corrosion.

B. Spring free length.

C. Spring open and close pressure.

D. All of the above.

19. Valve spring _____ overcomes valve train inertia and closes the valve at the appropriate time.

20. Valve stems and guides must be measured to check for _____ and   20. _____
_____.

21. What should you look for when inspecting a four-stroke engine valve seat and face?

_____

_____

22. A four-stroke engine cylinder head can be checked for warpage by   22. _____
    using all the following tools, EXCEPT:

    A. feeler gauge.

    B. Plastigage.

    C. straightedge.

    D. surface plate.

23. Describe the steps needed to recondition a four-stroke cylinder head assembly.

_____

_____

_____

_____

_____

24. Explain what should be done if a valve's margin is too thin after grinding.

_____

_____

25. Which of the following are valve face angles used on most   25. _____
    motorcycles?

    A. 30°.

    B. 45°.

    C. 75°.

    D. Both A & B.

26. What is the purpose of a valve seat *interference angle?*

_____

_____

27. Name and explain four important conditions to consider when refacing a valve seat.

_____

_____

_____

_____

_____

28. _____ determines seat pressure and spring tension throughout the   28. _____
    valve's travel.

Name _____

29. Identify the following four-stroke engine top end reassembly procedure.

_____

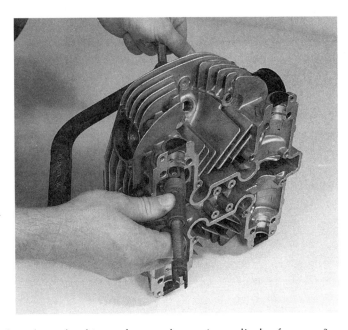

30. What should you look for when checking a four-stroke engine cylinder for wear?

_____

_____

31. Explain the important aspects to remember when measuring a four-stroke engine cylinder for wear.

_____

_____

_____

32. If an engine cylinder diameter equals 2.448″ and the piston diameter equals 2.444″, what does the piston clearance equal?

_____

_____

33. Define the term *ring-to-groove clearance.*

_____

_____

34. What type of measuring tool should be used to measure piston ring end gap?

_____

_____

35. What should be done if a four-stroke engine's connecting rod's small end diameter is beyond specifications but wrist pin diameter is correct?

_____

_____

36. Explain the procedure to follow if an engine cylinder is worn beyond service limits.

_____

_____

_____

37. An engine cylinder that has been honed or deglazed must be   37. _____
    washed in _____ to remove grit and metal particles.

Engine Bottom End Service

---

38. Name the parts that make up a four-stroke motorcycle engine bottom end.

_____

_____

_____

_____

39. List the four types of bearings found in four-stroke cycle engines.

_____

_____

_____

40. What should you look for when inspecting four-stroke cycle bearings?

_____

_____

_____

41. Name some of the four-stroke engine bottom end lubrication system components that require cleaning or
    replacement during an engine overhaul.

_____

_____

_____

42. List some of the questions that should be asked when diagnosing four-stroke engine lubrication system
    problems.

_____

_____

_____

_____

_____

_____

Name _____

43. Identify the parts and instruments involved in this four-stroke cycle
engine crankshaft measurement.

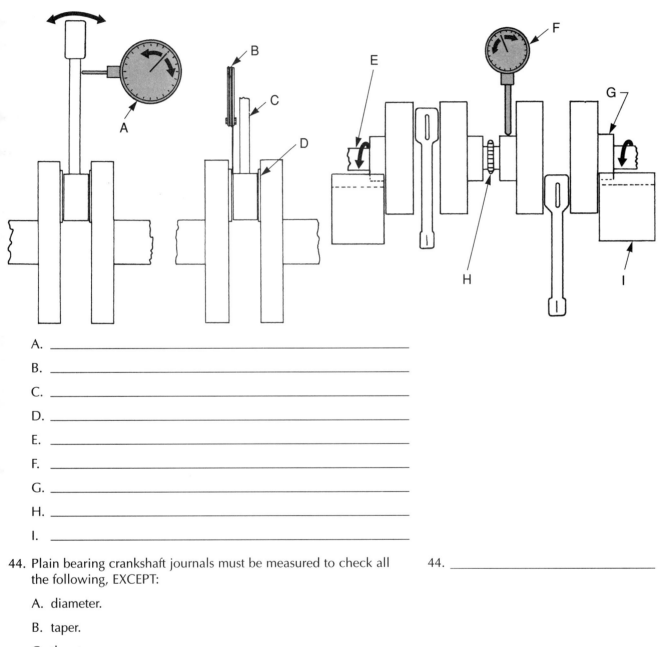

A. _____

B. _____

C. _____

D. _____

E. _____

F. _____

G. _____

H. _____

I. _____

44. Plain bearing crankshaft journals must be measured to check all
the following, EXCEPT:

    A. diameter.

    B. taper.

    C. thrust wear.

    D. out-of-roundness.

44. _____

45. List two ways to recondition a worn plain bearing crankshaft.

_____

_____

_____

46. When crankshaft journals measure within service limits and have a
smooth _____, they may be polished with _____ and reused.

46. _____

47. Describe what is done in *major crankshaft reconditioning.*

_____

_____

_____

48. Explain what to look for if there is uneven wear on the sides of a four-stroke engine piston or angled wear marks on the skirt.

_____

_____

49. Name some of the important steps to follow when overhauling a four-stroke engine bottom end.

_____

_____

_____

_____

_____

_____

50. Describe five major procedures to follow when inspecting a four-stroke motorcycle engine's oil pump.

_____

_____

_____

_____

Four-Stroke Engine Reassembly

51. Final main bearing assembly is completed when the _____ are   51. _____
    bolted together.

52. Why should engine components be lubricated during reassembly?

_____

_____

_____

53. Machined surfaces which do not use a gasket must be sealed with   53. _____
    a(n) _____.

54. Why must a proper torque pattern be used on a four-stroke motorcycle engine's cylinder, cylinder head, and crankcase castings?

_____

_____

_____

Name _____

55. Explain the importance of installing piston rings correctly.

_____

_____

_____

56. What rules should be remembered when installing engine piston rings?

_____

_____

_____

_____

_____

57. A(n) _____ is usually cast or stamped into the crown to indicate   57. _____
    piston direction.

58. Explain the important steps to follow when installing a four-stroke motorcycle engine cylinder.

_____

_____

_____

_____

59. Identify the following four-stroke motorcycle engine reassembly procedure.

_____

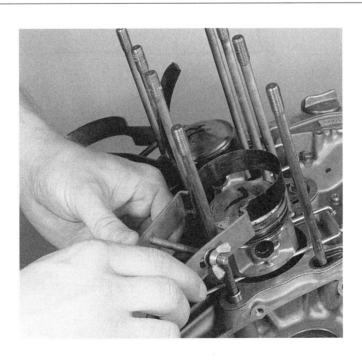

60. _____ determines valve movement in relation to piston movement.

60. _____

61. Name seven important steps to follow when installing a four-stroke motorcycle engine on its frame.

_____

_____

_____

_____

_____

_____

_____

62. After an engine overhaul, why should you make sure a four-stroke engine's lubrication system works properly?

_____

_____

_____

63. Name five inspection procedures to perform during four-stroke engine initial operation.

_____

_____

_____

_____

64. The break-in period of a four-stroke engine is very critical to _____ and _____.

64. _____

65. What is a typical break-in period for a four-stroke motorcycle engine?

_____

_____

66. List six rules to follow during four-stroke engine break-in.

_____

_____

_____

_____

_____

67. The _____ process of a four-stroke engine is a controlled wearing in of engine parts.

67. _____

68. As engine parts wear from _____ and gaskets settle from _____ and _____, part clearances may change.

68. _____

Name _____

69. How much mileage is needed for the initial seating of engine
    parts?

    69. _____

    A. 200-500 miles (322-806 km).

    B. 1000-2000 miles (1600-3220 km).

    C. 1500 miles (2413 km).

    D. 500 miles (800 km).

70. Why should you change the engine's oil and filter after the initial break-in period?

    _____

    _____

    _____

21

Power Transmission Overhaul

Objective: After studying this chapter, you will be able to inspect and overhaul a motorcycle clutch primary drive, transmission, and final drive. Also, you will be able to explain common motorcycle transmission problems.

Instructions: After studying the textbook, answer the workbook questions.

Primary Drive Service and Repair

1. What is the function of a motorcycle primary drive transmission?

_____

_____

_____

2. Define the term *external chain primary drive.*

_____

_____

_____

3. An external chain primary drive requires overhaul when the   3. _____
   _____ or _____ becomes worn or broken.

4. Name a symptom of a loose primary drive chain.

_____

_____

_____

5. What is indicated if there is no adjustment left on the primary drive chain tensioner?

_____

_____

6. An internal chain drive's primary drive chain is located at the _____ of the motorcycle engine crankshaft.

6. _____

7. What should you look for when inspecting the condition of an external gear primary drive?

_____

_____

8. Measurement of primary drive gear backlash identifies minor wear of the _____.

8. _____

9. The internal gear primary drive is housed within the _____.

9. _____

Clutch Service and Repair

10. Name some of the causes of motorcycle clutch wear and failure.

_____

_____

_____

11. List some of the motorcycle clutch components that can wear and fail.

_____

_____

_____

_____

12. Which of the following is *not* a location of clutch basket and bearing wear?

12. _____

    A. Basket fingers.

    B. Basket gear.

    C. Basket cushion.

    D. Center bearing thrust washer.

13. What should an inspection of a motorcycle's friction plates include?

_____

_____

_____

_____

14. Describe what an inspection of a motorcycle clutch plain plates should include.

_____

_____

_____

Name _____

15. Explain the purpose of motorcycle clutch springs.

_____

_____

16. Name four common causes of inadequate clutch spring pressure and clutch slippage.

_____

_____

_____

_____

17. How is clutch spring condition determined?

_____

_____

18. What does *truing* of a motorcycle clutch pressure plate assembly involve?

_____

_____

19. A kickstart mechanism that works through the clutch is called a(n)   19. _____

_____.

20. What should a chain primary drive inspection consist of?

_____

_____

_____

21. What should you look for when inspecting the condition of a motorcycle clutch basket?

_____

_____

_____

_____

22. What should a clutch hub inspection include?

_____

_____

_____

23. List some of the parts that should be checked during a primary kickstart inspection.

_____

_____

_____

Transmission Service and Repair

24. Which of the following is a common motorcycle transmission   24. _____
    problem?

    A. Jumping out of gear.

    B. Transmission locked up.

    C. Missing gear ratio.

    D. All of the above.

25. What procedures should be performed before disassembling a motorcycle transmission?

    _____

    _____

    _____

26. Identify the following transmission service procedure.

    _____

27. What should you look for when inspecting a motorcycle   27. _____
    transmission shift mechanism?

    A. Freedom of movement.

    B. Proper adjustment for the shift stopper pin.

    C. Worn pivots in the shift arm.

    D. All of the above.

Name _____

28. Why is it important to disassemble one transmission shaft assembly at a time during transmission teardown?

_____

_____

_____

29. What problems should you look for when transmission disassembly has been completed?

_____

_____

_____

_____

_____

_____

30. List the three measurements that are very critical to the overhaul of a motorcycle transmission.

_____

_____

_____

_____

31. Name some of the problems that can occur with a motorcycle kickstart mechanism.

_____

_____

_____

_____

32. Describe the four variations in motorcycle transmission mounting.

_____

_____

_____

_____

_____

33. Which of the following is used to check transmission shaft end play   33. _____
    in order to adjust shimming?

    A. External measurement using a dial indicator.

    B. Internal measurement.

    C. External measurement using Plastigage.

    D. Both A & B.

34. Describe how to adjust external end play on a motorcycle transmission.

_____

_____

_____

_____

35. What does transmission internal end play measurement normally involve?

_____

_____

_____

_____

Final Drive Service and Repair

36. Name some of the normal maintenance procedures required for a chain drive system.

_____

_____

_____

_____

37. Name two methods in which a chain drive may be lubricated.

_____

_____

38. Chain adjustment is the positioning of the _____ and _____ to   38. _____
    provide proper free play and alignment.

39. Why shouldn't you inspect the drive chain while the motorcycle engine is running?

_____

_____

_____

_____

40. What is the most common method of adjusting a motorcycle drive chain?

_____

_____

_____

_____

Name _____

41. Identify the parts and designated markings encountered during chain drive adjustment.

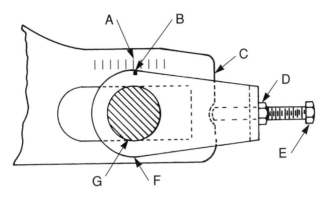

A. _____

B. _____

C. _____

D. _____

E. _____

F. _____

G. _____

42. While adjusting chain free play, you should always check for any _____ caused by uneven chain or sprocket wear.

42. _____

43. A new _____ should be installed in the axle nut following chain adjustment.

43. _____

44. What service procedure should be performed if a motorcycle's drive chain is dry, kinked, or rusted?

_____

_____

45. Explain the term *chain stretch.*

_____

_____

46. What service procedure should be performed if a motorcycle's drive chain and sprockets are worn?

_____

_____

47. A drive belt is often used in place of a chain on some _____ transmissions.

47. _____

48. What should you look for when inspecting the condition of a drive belt?

_____

_____

49. What should be checked before belt installation?

_____

_____

50. What is indicated if an ATV equipped with a drive belt system   50. _____
    engine starts but the vehicle will not move?

    A. Worn drive belt.

    B. Damaged ramp plate.

    C. Worn or damaged clutch lining.

    D. All of the above.

51. A vehicle equipped with a drive belt system has poor performance at high speeds. Describe some of the possible causes of this problem.

_____

_____

52. Name some of the typical inspection and maintenance operations normally performed on a shaft final drive unit.

_____

_____

_____

53. Describe this rear drive unit service procedure and label the names of the tools and operations involved.

_____

_____

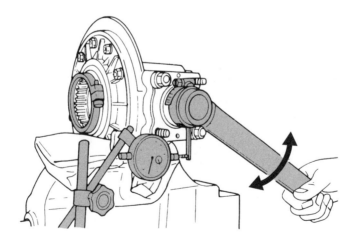

Name _____

54. What should be the first steps to follow during rear drive unit removal?

_____

_____

55. Describe what a rear drive unit inspection should consist of.

_____

_____

_____

_____

56. When adjusting ring and pinion gear backlash on a rear drive unit,   56. _____
_____ are used to move the ring gear into or away from the
pinion gear.

57. List the steps to follow when checking a rear drive unit's ring and pinion tooth contact pattern.

_____

_____

_____

_____

_____

58. Explain some of the causes of excessive noise in a shaft final drive unit.

_____

_____

_____

_____

59. There is excessive noise in a shaft final drive unit side gear. Name some of the possible problems.

_____

_____

_____

60. List three causes of an oil leak at a shaft final drive's gear case.

_____

_____

_____

Name _____

Date _____

Instructor _____

Period _____ Text pages 485-506

22

Tune-Up and General Service

Objective: After studying this chapter, you will be able to perform a complete motorcycle engine tune-up which includes ignition system, fuel system, and valve train adjustment. You will also be able to describe common motorcycle service procedures.

Instructions: After studying the textbook, answer the workbook questions.

Inspection

1. A motorcycle engine should be in good _____ before attempting a tune-up.

   1. _____

2. What should you check first when beginning a tune up or other service work on a computer-controlled bike?

   _____

   _____

3. Describe how to inspect and replace a motorcycle air filter.

   _____

   _____

   _____

   _____

4. Which of the following is *not* a step in replacing a motorcycle fuel filter?

   4. _____

   A. Drain the fuel tank.

   B. Shut off the fuel petcock.

   C. Relieve fuel system pressure.

   D. Replace the fuel filter.

5. Identify some of the motorcycle components that should be inspected during servicing.

A. _____   E. _____

B. _____   F. _____

C. _____   G. _____

D. _____   H. _____

Battery Service

6. What should be inspected when checking the condition of a motorcycle battery?

_____

_____

_____

_____

Name _____

Checking Cooling System

7. When checking a liquid-cooled motorcycle engine's cooling system, you should use a(n) _____ to test coolant concentration.

7. _____

8. Servicing air-cooled motorcycle engines is limited to making sure the _____ are free of dirt and debris and are not damaged.

8. _____

Engine and Chassis Lubrication

9. Name some of the parts that should be lubricated during motorcycle servicing.

_____

_____

_____

Tire and Wheel Service

10. Explain what to look for when checking the condition of a motorcycle's tires.

_____

_____

_____

11. A motorcycle's front spoked wheel has very slight runout. How can this problem be corrected?

_____

_____

_____

Replacing Spark Plugs

12. What should be done *next* after removing the spark plug from the engine?

_____

_____

_____

13. When installing a spark plug in an aluminum cylinder head, the spark plug threads should be coated with _____ or _____.

13. _____

14. Identify the following spark plug service procedure.

_____

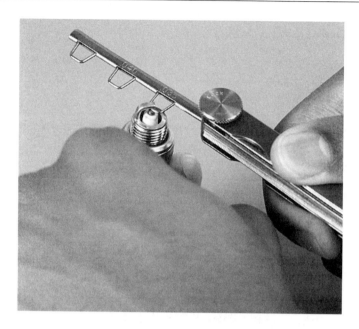

Measuring Engine Compression and Leak-Down

15. Describe the function of a motorcycle engine compression test.

_____

_____

_____

_____

16. Compression test readings 10% or more above specification may indicate _____ is raising the compression ratio.

16. _____

17. A wet compression test is performed on a motorcycle engine. The compression readings increased to more than the previous readings. What problems are indicated?

17. _____

    A. Hole in the piston.

    B. Worn cylinder and/or piston rings.

    C. Worn bearing.

    D. Improper fuel mixture.

18. The crankcase primary compression is too low in a two-stroke motorcycle engine. Name some of the possible causes of this problem.

_____

_____

_____

Name _____

19. What are the applications of a cylinder leak-down test?

_____

_____

_____

20. Why is regular crankcase leak-down testing very important to the lifespan of a two-stroke engine?

_____

_____

_____

21. Describe how to perform a two-stroke cycle engine crankcase leak test.

_____

_____

_____

_____

_____

Ignition System Tune-Up

22. What does contact point ignition system service involve?

_____

_____

_____

_____

23. Heavy contact point pitting or erosion usually indicates the need   23. _____
    for _____ replacement.

24. How does rubbing block wear affect the performance of a contact point ignition system?

_____

_____

_____

_____

25. _____ is the amount of clearance between the contact surfaces   25. _____
    when they are wide open.

26. _____ is the amount of time in crankshaft degrees the contacts are   26. _____
    closed.

27. Identify the following contact point ignition system service procedure.

_____

===
Ignition Timing Adjustment
===

28. Ignition timing refers to the _____ and _____ position when the   28. _____
    spark occurs.

29. How is ignition timing normally checked?

    _____

    _____

    _____

30. Name the three methods used to alter ignition timing.

    _____

    _____

    _____

31. Static ignition timing adjustment is done without the _____ and   31. _____
    with the ignition switch in the _____ position.

32. Define the term *static timing*.

    _____

    _____

Name _____

33. A(n) _____ triggered by the secondary ignition circuit is used to check dynamic timing.

33. _____

34. Why is dynamic timing more accurate than static timing?

_____

_____

_____

35. Contact points have been installed in a motorcycle engine. Which timing adjustment procedure should be performed *first?*

35. _____

   A. Dynamic timing.

   B. Static timing.

   C. Centrifugal advance.

   D. None of the above.

Electronic Ignition System Service

36. Identify the parts on this electronic ignition system.

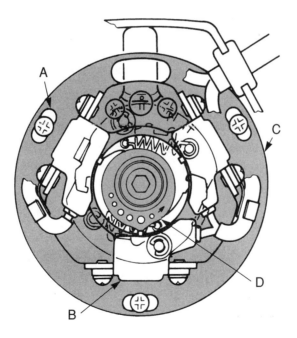

A. _____

B. _____

C. _____

D. _____

37. How is the *air gap* adjusted and set on an electronic ignition system?

_____

_____

_____

Engine and Carburetor Tune-Up

38. How can changes in valve clearance due to normal wear be corrected?

_____

_____

_____

39. How can a loose cam chain affect motorcycle engine performance?

_____

_____

_____

_____

40. _____ is a very fine modification of the carburetor's air-fuel mixture at idle and slightly above.

40. _____

41. Name two motorcycle engine tune-up service procedures which may affect carburetor settings.

_____

_____

_____

42. _____ is the adjustment of the throttles to achieve equal air-fuel delivery to each cylinder.

42. _____

43. What is the recommended idle speeds for most motorcycle carburetors?

43. _____

Tune-Up and General Service Summary

44. What is the importance of a motorcycle periodic maintenance chart?

_____

_____

_____

_____

Name _____

45. Why should a motorcycle service department keep neat and accurate documentation of all repairs performed on each vehicle?

_____

_____

_____

_____

_____

_____

_____

_____

23

The Business of Motorcycle, ATV, and Scooter Service

Objective: After studying this chapter, you will be able to describe the various career opportunities and job classifications available to successful motorcycle technicians. You will also learn how to properly prepare a bike for storage and inspect and correct motorcycle safety related problems.

Instructions: After studying the textbook, answer the workbook questions.

Employment in the Motorcycle Industry

1. The motorcycle dealership is the major link between the _____ and the _____.

   1. _____

2. Define the term *dealership.*

   _____

   _____

   _____

   _____

3. A(n) _____ dealership is one that has signed a contract with a particular manufacturer to sell and service a particular line of motorcycles.

   3. _____

4. The motorcycle dealership's sales and service policies are usually set by the _____.

   4. _____

5. _____ service a variety of motorcycles, ATVs, and scooters without being contractually limited to any particular manufacturer's line of vehicles.

   5. _____

Job Classifications

6. What are the responsibilities of a motorcycle service technician?

_____

_____

_____

_____

7. What are the essential qualifications for a motorcycle dealership or shop service writer?

_____

_____

_____

_____

8. Who in the motorcycle dealership or shop is responsible for maintaining a set inventory of commonly-used parts, such as filters, belts, hoses, fasteners, and gaskets?

_____

_____

_____

9. In a dealership, the _____ makes certain the motorcycle   9. _____
   manufacturers' policies concerning warranties, service procedures,
   and customer relations are carried out.

10. Describe the responsibilities of a motorcycle parts sales representative.

_____

_____

_____

_____

Storage

11. What normally happens to a motorcycle that sits for a prolonged period of time?

_____

_____

_____

_____

Name _____

12. Which of the following should *not* be done when returning a motorcycle to service after storage?

    A. Remove spark plugs or vapor plugs and turn the engine over several times.

    B. Take the bike on a thorough road test to its performance limits.

    C. Rinse with fresh fuel, and clean the filter screen.

    D. Check, adjust, and lubricate all cables and drive chains.

12. _____

Liability

13. Define the term *liability*.

_____

_____

_____

_____

14. Describe some of the conditions that can make a motorcycle unsafe.

_____

_____

_____

_____

15. A(n) _____ occurs if a possible safety defect or other problem is discovered in a certain vehicle model.

15. _____

16. What does a motorcycle, ATV, or scooter safety check normally involve?

_____

_____

_____

_____

_____

_____

_____

_____

17. Describe the purpose of the following form.

_____

_____

_____

_____

NAME OF SHOP

123 West Taft
Tinley Park, IL   60473

From: _____

To: _____

THIS MOTORCYCLE NEEDS _____

_____

_____

TO BE ROADWORTHY, THE CUSTOMER/
OWNER ACCEPTS THE MOTORCYCLE AS IS
AND ACCEPTS ALL RESPONSIBILITY FOR ITS
UNSAFE CONDITION.

Signature _____

Warranty

18. What are the warranty related questions that should be asked when a motorcycle, ATV, or scooter comes in for service?

_____

_____

_____

Working in the Field

19. What is the most important skill a motorcycle technician should develop?

_____

_____

_____

Name _____

20. As a technician, what are the rewards for being known as a "sure finisher" in the motorcycle dealership or service shop?

_____

_____

_____

_____

_____

_____